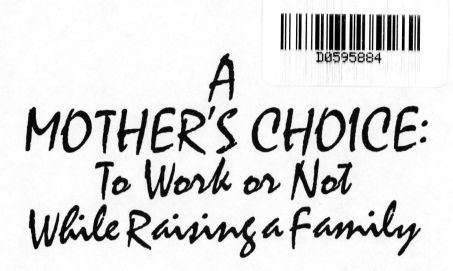

A MOTHER'S CHOICE:
To Work or Not While Raising a Family

BARBARA ENSOR COOK

BETTERWAY PUBLICATIONS, INC.
WHITE HALL, VIRGINIA

Published by Betterway Publications, Inc.
Box 219
Crozet, VA 22932

Cover design by Deborah B. Chappell

Library of Congress Cataloging in Publication Data

Cook, Barbara Ensor
    A Mother's Choice

    Includes index.
    1. Working mothers—United States.   2. Work and family—United States.   I. Title
HQ759.48.C66   1988   306.8'7   88-2529
ISBN 0-932620-95-7 (pbk.)

Printed in the United States of America
9 8 7 6 5 4 3 2 1

To Tara,
May your choice be easier; and
to David and Brian,
the men in our lives.

My appreciation goes to the women who were interviewed for this project. Most of them were strangers; a few were friends. They were open and candid about some very personal areas in their lives.

Sharon Maybarduk, my research assistant, was of invaluable assistance in making numerous trips to the library and tracking down hard-to-find publications. She conducted many of the interviews and located some "hot prospects" on her own. Her help made this book a manageable task in light of my own juggling of personal and professional responsibilities at the time.

My family was kind enough to allow me to appropriate the dining room table for seven months and to permit "the book" to occasionally encroach upon our time together.

Contents

Introduction: The Big Choice

There are many big choices to make throughout one's life: where to attend school, which type of career to pursue, whether or not to get married (and to whom), whether or not to have children (and how many), where to live, when to retire, etc.

For mothers of children under eighteen, the big choice that can dominate years of decision making revolves around whether to work while raising a family. Like most critical choices, it touches many areas of our lives. A choice to work may limit the number of children you can parent effectively. A choice not to work may affect your standard of living tremendously.

One thing is certain. Society has not made this an easy choice for us. The support systems that helped our mothers no longer are available to most of us. While new ideas are emerging to cope with our changing society, we have not yet institutionalized them sufficiently to create stability.

Many sociologists, psychologists, and economists have suggested that the most outstanding phenomenon of our century is the huge number of women entering the labor force. The effects of the sociological upheaval will not be analyzed properly for decades. We do know that we are charting new territory. The issue involves much more than working mothers, which is not an idea born with this generation of women.

What is new is that more than half of American families now rely on two incomes to pay their bills. Children of working mothers, in increasingly larger numbers and at increasingly younger ages, are being left for much of the day with nonfamily members. Professional opportunities now available to women were unthinkable for the generation that came before us. Yet there has never been so little support from so many quarters for the choices we make.

The array of choices facing women is both exciting and unsettling. The purpose of this book is to look at the options that are available to us and to explore a method of decision making. My hope is to enable you to make a wise choice which yields a sense of peace. The "big choice" is one that may need constant reevaluation as family needs change.

It also should be pointed out that there are many women who have no choice regarding employment. Their decisions are dictated by circumstances. Yet I believe there are large numbers who claim to be ruled by circumstances, but in fact have chosen the most obvious or easiest (but not necessarily wisest) route.

This book is addressed, without apologies, to women. There is indeed evidence that male-female roles are changing. Our husbands are taking more active roles in family life than our fathers did. However, the fact remains that most fathers expect to work full time for the majority of the years that dependent children are in the home. Conversely, I cannot think of a mother I know who has not agonized about her decision to work, and how it will affect her future and that of her loved ones.

Throughout the next several chapters, you will meet mothers from all parts of the country with children living at home. Some have chosen to be homemakers; others are employed part or full time. Many have changed directions several times. Some are happy; some are not. Some worry about the future; some are consumed with today's problems. The joys and concerns they express probably echo your own, or those of someone you know.

My own choices have been varied. When my first child was born, I stayed at home for one year while completing graduate school. For many years, I worked part time. My work schedule slowly increased to the point that as my younger child entered school last year, I found myself temporarily juggling three part-time professional commitments totaling more than a full-time workload. I finally settled down into one full-time job.

While I have been an advocate of part-time employment for many years, I do not believe it is the best option for all mothers at all stages of their lives. I have met both homemakers and employed women who are satisfied that what they have chosen is best for their families. Clearly, I can offer you no easy answer to a complicated question. I do offer a thorough look at what should go into your thought process as you decide whether or not to work while your children are at home.

Your choice *is* critical. It will affect your financial status, your career, your family life and your relationships with others. In fact, the enormity of the consequences is what causes so many women to question constantly if they have made the right choice. So take the time to consider the following chapters and make a wise decision for your "big choice."

1.
A New Choice

Looking back at my life for the past eight years, I liken it to skydiving. I feel as though I were tossed from an airplane and somehow, miraculously, landed on my feet. Despite a faulty parachute and belated steering, I managed to land safely, but I was definitely not prepared for my leap.

A GENERATION UNPREPARED

Ever since I can remember, I thought I would get married and have a couple of children. In addition, I assumed I would have an interesting career of some sort. Like many women my age, I guessed that everything would fall into place when the time came. When the time did come, I found that babies and jobs were both hard work, and that nothing fell into place without an inordinate amount of effort on my part.

I didn't plan ahead for the big choice. It was not until I was confronted with immediate problems and issues that I learned not only how to make a wise decision, but also how to predict and plan for the future choices.

I was born in 1950. In one sense, this gives me a marvelous vantage point. I look ahead at mothers ten years older than I and see, for the most part, women who left the work force without question with the advent of children. As their children grew, they faced the dilemma of how and when to reenter the labor force. Few of them will remain homemakers as did most of their mothers.

As I look over my shoulder at women ten years my junior, my vision is one of mothers who are economically unable and also scared to death to leave their jobs. Knowing that they will need to work for a majority of their lives, they hesitate to give up or postpone their careers. Therefore, they try to balance two jobs. Yet, just as our children eventually learn the sad truth

11

about Santa Claus, the Easter Bunny, and the Tooth Fairy, young mothers find out that Superwoman is a myth. It is not as easy as they tell us and yes, we do need to make choices.

Being in my mid-thirties also has placed me in the eye of the hurricane. Everything changed so quickly around us that we did not have time to get our bearings; role models were nonexistent and expectations limitless. Suddenly the options were all there, but we were a bit reluctant to turn ourselves or our children into test cases. And yet we did.

Fortunately I have survived the first round of choices of the work and parenting issue. My children are now school-aged, and part of me sits back with a huge sigh of relief. I have developed marketable skills in three distinct career fields, and feel that interesting possibilities are open to me. I do not feel that I have "lost ground" with other professionals my age. At the same time, my husband and I have been the primary caretakers and influence in our children's lives.

Another part of me is angry, however, that there has been so little help or guidance along the way. I am not even sure where the anger is directed. Is it at high school and college guidance counselors who give little or no practical direction in what comes after all of those courses are finished? Is it at the business community, which is absorbing huge numbers of mothers into the work force, yet expects them to function as though they had wives at home? Is it at men in general, who may or may not help with household and child care responsibilities, seldom equally share them, and almost never face the big choice? Or is it directed at women, who spend more time explaining and defending their choices than helping each other to get through it all. Maybe it is just at society, which for years has recognized the problems, but has decided to invest its resources elsewhere.

THE INSTITUTION OF MOTHERHOOD

As we analyze the changes in our way of living, often we shortsightedly and nostalgically compare it with what we remember one generation ago. The Cleavers, the Nelsons, and the Andersons showed us what family life was meant to be. June, Harriet, and Margaret never talked about child care or when to return to work. Is my generation of mothers so unique in confronting this decision to pursue a career while effectively providing care to our children?

Yes and no. Yes, I believe the environment in which we live has never been the norm previously in our country's history.

Some of these factors which have become commonplace to our generation are the following:

- Second incomes being utilized not for luxuries, but necessities in many cases.
- Huge numbers of single-parent families, primarily headed by women.
- Institutionalized care and care by nonfamily members of children.
- Isolation of homemakers from other adults and lack of support systems for all kinds of mothers.

No, we are not the first generation of women to work and mother simultaneously. In *The Future of Motherhood*, Dr. Jessie Bernard makes the case that it is the creation of "mother" as an occupation that is new. This recent phenomenon is the result of an affluent society. Throughout history and still in most of the world today, women can not be spared to give the majority of their time and efforts to raising children.

One study of 86 societies throughout the world yielded interesting results. Less than one-half (46 percent) of the mothers were the primary or exclusive caretakers of infants. Approximately 40 percent of the infants were cared for by older children, usually siblings. The rate was even lower for children past infancy. Mothers were the primary or exclusive caretakers only 20 percent of the time.[1]

When our nation was young, most families worked as units either on the farm or in the home providing goods or services. Women worked in the home and on the land in a family economy which was basically self-sufficient in terms of food, clothing, and shelter. Their work was complementary to tasks performed by men. Children worked in some capacity from the time they were physically able. Until well into the 1900s, physical chores took up most of a woman's day.[2] I wonder if they ever worried about quality time?

The Industrial Revolution brought the first sweeping changes to the manner in which families worked. With the advent of factories, large numbers of workers left the home to earn a living. Men took the first jobs in machine production. The number of skilled craftsmen slowly began to diminish. "Work" began to mean "labor in the marketplace." In some cases, entire families went off to work together. Spinners in textile mills often brought along their wives and children as young as eight or nine years old as assistants.[3] Until modern management systems took hold in the 1890s, the family was seen as the natural way for businesses to recruit new labor.

Many women remained in the home as men went off to work. Technology made household chores less time consuming. The first factory to transform raw cotton to a finished cloth product was established in 1813. By 1830, the majority of spinning and weaving was being performed in factories, thus eliminating the home manufacture of cloth for clothing and household use.[4] As the century progressed, there were many advances in the preparation of food. New sources of water, energy, and light also eased many household chores. In addition, as the public school system began to reach most communities, the duty of educating children was removed from the home.

In the nineteenth century, most older children worked to supplement the family income. Child labor laws and educational reform slowly removed this source of labor by the turn of the century. Some of the void was filled by women, By this time, most women left the home reluctantly.[5] The type of work which was available to them was not appealing and the message of society was to stay at home and be mothers.

A slow, but definite change in thinking began to differentiate working women from ladies. The earliest group of women employed outside of the home were the "mill girls" in the early 1800s. Many viewed their employment as a temporary necessity which would provide them with independence and money until marriage. In the second part of the century, women moved into many areas of manufacturing, including the production of boots and shoes, food-related items, cigars, boxes, etc. Whenever possible, women viewed marriage as an escape from this type of labor.

Other employment options were equally unappealing. By 1900, the average female worker was likely to be found in domestic service, as a maid, cook, laundress, or nurse. Some worked long hours, six days a week, in retail trade and restaurants. Professional women were an oddity. No wonder women longed to be middle-class housewives. Married women who needed to earn money tried their best to hide the fact from the public eye.[6]

By the turn of the century, working was unthinkable for respectable married women. Girls from proper families were limited to certain types of acceptable jobs for brief stints before marriage. In 1910, only five percent of white, married women were employed.[7] Women with time on their hands were expected to join clubs or donate their time to worthwhile volunteer pursuits.

Those women who did not join the work force increased the time they spent mothering. An interesting, hundred-year study of the *Ladies Home Journal* revealed that this boost to the occupation of motherhood came mainly from the business community, anxious to sell the latest technology.[8] The message of the advertisements was, "Use our products and you will have time for your children, whose care should not be entrusted to servants."

As early as 1830, child-rearing manuals and periodicals were published. Mother was extolled as the primary influence and molder of her children's futures. Father was barely mentioned. The basic premise of the publications was that child care was the exclusive domain of the mother, and therefore should be her primary job.

Like many social phenomena, child-rearing attitudes shift as a pendulum swings back and forth. The role set aside for Mother in the twentieth century was decried as "smother love" in the 1920s and 1930s. Psychologist John Watson, author of *Psychological Care of Infant and Child,* blamed indulgent, demonstrative mothers for "ruining the youth of America."[9] According to experts, children should be kept to strict schedules and treated as miniature adults. Women were encouraged to invest their time elsewhere, in hobbies, not jobs.

Twenty years later, the pendulum had once again shifted to the other side. Dr. Spock, now labeled as the father of permissive parenting, said that babies knew best when they were hungry or tired. In allowing the infant to self-schedule, mothers found they had given up control of the daily regimen. Once again, they were encouraged to devote undivided attention to their offspring.

Meanwhile, the household technology which made work more efficient and saved labor, did not necessarily save time. Jessie Bernard writes that like Parkinson's law, the work increased to fill the available hours. Improvements mandated a higher standard of housekeeping, too. People wanted clean clothes every day, not every week. More was expected in the way of meal preparation and household cleanliness.[10]

In the 1880s, scientists discovered that disease was caused by germs, not "bad" air. Now there was a new enemy to fight on the household front. An interesting twist was that just as servants were beginning to become a scarce commodity, they were labeled as sources of contagion, as well as one more mouth to feed.[11]

Amidst changes in child-rearing techniques and household technology, Mother certainly ruled the home for several decades. At the turn of the century, wealthy women supervised a household of servants in addition to raising several children. If Mother were poor, she was a servant or worked in a factory or store. If she fell somewhere in between, she probably did her own housework and if necessary, used her skills to supplement the family income from her home.

By the middle of the twentieth century, a homemaker's main duties had developed into mothering, housework, shopping and a new chore, chauffeuring. By now, only the extremely wealthy could afford daily household help. Most of this labor pool had found better opportunities in office work, and the cost of domestic help rose dramatically.

One exception to women's employment history was manifested in times of war. During the Civil War, women managed plantations, farms, and businesses when their husbands went off to fight. Women were also utilized during World War I. Only a minority of employed women went into the war industries; most sought skilled positions being vacated by soldiers.

Throughout the long, draining years of the second World War, Rosie the Riveter became a national heroine. Leaving the home was not only understood, but considered a patriotic duty. Child care programs sprang up overnight, financed by federal funds.[12]

As quickly as the programs were set up, they were dismantled after the war was over. Despite studies conducted near the end of the war which indicated that 80 percent of women wanted to continue working, a national propaganda campaign urged them to return to the home, giving up their jobs to veterans.[13] Many were fired to make room for men. Those who needed to work returned to traditional female occupations. The rest settled down in mushrooming suburbs, bought houses, had three or four babies, and lived happily ever after.

Almost. Somewhere along the line, the troops got restless. By the 1960s, the boredom, frustration, and anger exploded into the women's movement. Women began to return to the labor force, slowly at first, and by the 1970s, in record numbers. In the 1980s, mothers with children under six years old have become the fastest growing segment of the work force. Painful steps were taken to redefine roles for both men and women. The excesses of a minority created the inevitable reactionary backlash. The battle lines were drawn.

UNDER ATTACK

In the midst of all these changes, the occupation of motherhood fell lower and lower on the status scale. In her book, *The New Suburban Woman,* Nancy Rubin explores the paradox of the message that today's woman receives from society regarding motherhood: it is sacred, but worthless. She cites several reasons for the devaluation of motherhood:

- Improved birth control methods mean fewer children.

- Lower infant and child mortality rates make it unnecessary to have a large number of babies in order for two or three to survive to adulthood.

- Children have transformed from an economic advantage to a burden.

- Children are controlled more by schools, peers, and the media, and less by family.

- Women have increased educational and career opportunities.

- The economy has forced many women into the labor market.

- Feminism has preached that women are human beings, not reproductive vessels.[14]

RUSH TO THE WORKPLACE

In short, there is less to do around the home and more to do in the outside world. The work that is done in the home has no monetary value and little prestige in contemporary society. Therefore, work in the "real world" is seen as more glamorous, even though this may be far from the truth for many jobs.

In addition to the social pressures, there are certainly economic incentives for working, not raising babies. Many families can not feed those babies unless mothers work. The average woman can expect to spend more than one-half of her adult life to age 65 working. A break in labor force participation can mean much more than simply the lost income and benefits for those years. It could mean giving up a job she may not be able to get back or losing promotional opportunities, pension rights, and seniority.

In the face of these various obstacles, what woman would choose to remain at home for an extended period of time? I suppose one who has fallen in love with her baby and is reluctant to be parted from him or her for much of the child's waking hours. One who feels that imparting values can not be entrusted to a substitute caregiver, particularly a nonfamily member. One who does not want to hear second hand about first steps, and later on, how things went at school that day.

And therein lies the big choice.

LIFE PLANNING

For several years, I taught a course entitled "How to Juggle Work, Marriage, and Family." The initial portion of the class deals with work options, and how to decide the amount of time and manner in which to work. The lack of planning on the part of the participants became the impetus for this book. I saw women dealing with many issues and concerns that were unnecessary, but had been caused by poor decision making.

These women (and most other individuals I know, both male and female) seem to fall into one of three categories. One group, the "strugglers," are constantly reacting to crises. Life seems to be just one big wave after another destined to knock them down. It takes all of their efforts simply to survive. The "floaters" ride the waves wherever they may go. They make the best of the trip, but are seldom sure where they are headed. Finally, the "swimmers" choose to get from one point to another. Occasionally, nature may change their courses slightly, but they usually get where they want to go despite the waves.

Taking control over your life and where you are headed is possible for everyone. The degree of control may be influenced by available resources, other people or situations, or unforeseen circumstances. Life planning requires a few basic processes:

- Focus on which areas of your life need direction.

- Investigate and analyze the issue at hand.

- Make a decision about where you want to go.

- Initiate actions which will help you reach your goal.

- Evaluate along the way.

CONVERSATIONS ACROSS THE COUNTRY

Throughout this book, you will see how other mothers have made choices regarding employment. These women were interviewed specifically for this project. I could have written thousands of pages based on the conversations with women in my classes and others that I have met through my contacts through the Association of Part-Time Professionals. However, this is an admittedly biased group of women who have expressed a preference for part-time employment by their association membership or to a lesser degree, attendance at workshops and meetings.

For that matter, I could write an entire chapter on almost every woman I know, including casual acquaintances. Most conversations with mothers of children still living at home revolve around two major issues: how the children are developing, and what the mothers are doing as they grow. If the women are already employed, their concerns center on how to manage all of their responsibilities. If the women are not employed, they talk about when they will return to work and what type of job they will have.

I chose to interview forty women, some acquaintances, but mostly strangers, to capture their feelings about the big choice. Their comments and stories touched my heart and reaffirmed many of the convictions I had formed before I started this book. In some cases, I was surprised at my findings. Each woman was asked a standard set of 25 questions, and each set of answers was unique.

I didn't intend to gather statistical data, so my approach was not scientific. Instead I was interested in stories, feelings, anecdotes, beliefs, and questions. I also wanted most of the interviews to be away from the area where I live (the metropolitan Washington, DC area). Because Washington, DC has the highest labor force participation rate in the country for mothers of children under 18, I was afraid that women here might not accurately reflect the diverse attitude which exists in the country. On the other hand, most people living in the Washington, DC area were born and raised elsewhere, so it was very easy to locate a mixture of women even in my own back yard.

The only two conditions for interview candidates were that they be mothers, and still have at least one child under 18 residing in the home. The ages of the women ranged from mid-twenties to late forties. Their children (families consisted of one to seven children) ranged from infants to teenagers, with quite a few mothers pregnant. I tried to achieve a balance between women who had chosen to be homemakers, to work part time, and to work full time. There was also a near-equal split between professional and nonprofessional career women. Almost all of the women were currently married, because it is hard to find single parents who feel they have a great deal of choice about working.

After listening to many hours of tape, several times over, there were only a few areas of consensus I could pinpoint regarding the big choice:

- It was indeed big! It was something most women thought about in some way on a daily basis.

- There was little support and few role models to look to for guidance.

- The women felt unique as a generation. Few believed that their mothers understood their options or dilemmas.

- No one really had any answers yet. The changes have been too recent for us to evaluate the consequences of our actions.

Maybe we will be able to speak with more certainty to our daughters than to our friends. As one woman who had taken a full-time position recently stated rather eloquently:

"We are in the process of going through growing pains. Mothers working, part time or full time, have disrupted the family structure, there's no doubt about it.

"But what we need to do now is to take a look at the family and see how we maintain and keep the structure together. It's like any other law in the universe. You don't move and change one thing without affecting a multitude of other things. For every action, there is an equal and opposite reaction.

"What we have to do is go back and see how we can best keep the family together in light of these changes. That's what I want to do. Working will cause changes and we have to learn how to deal with them."

FOOTNOTES

[1]Maxine L. Margolis, *Mothers and Such* (Berkeley: University of California Press, 1984), p. 15.

[2]Karen Levine, "Mother vs. Mother," *Parents* (June, 1985), 60:6, p. 65.

[3]Rosabeth Moss Kanter, *Work and Family in the United States: A Critical Review and Agenda* (New York: Russell Sage Foundation, 1977), p. 10.

[4]Margolis, *op. cit.*, p. 117.

[5]Levine, *op. cit.*, p. 65.

[6]Susan Estabrook Kennedy, *If All We Did Was to Weep at Home: A History of White Working-Class Women in America* (Bloomington: Indiana University Press, 1979), p. 93.

[7]Margolis, *op. cit.*, p. 46

[8]Jessie Bernard, *The Future of Motherhood* (New York: The Dial Press, 1974), p. 125.

[9]Margolis, *op. cit.*, p. 58.

[10]Bernard, *op. cit.*, p. 126.

[11]Margolis, *op. cit.*, p. 128.

[12]Levine, *op. cit.*, p. 65.

[13]Kennedy, *op. cit.*, p. 197.

[14]Nancy Rubin, *The New Suburban Woman* (New York: Coward, McCann & Geoghegan, 1982), pp. 152-3.

2.
Battle Lines

At your next social gathering, eavesdrop on a few conversations or pay attention to your own. I can guess what you will hear, particularly if two women are talking. When two strangers meet, there are usually certain types of questions that are asked. They must be general and nonoffensive. Questions about age, weight, and money do not pass the latter test. In order to find specific topics of conversation where there is a common interest, you have to get through the initial general inquiries.

The three most common general inquiries are related to where the person currently lives or was raised, how he or she came to be at the gathering where you meet, and what the individual does for a living. This last question seems to enrage certain folks. I personally feel that it is a harmless, natural question. It is what comes next that bothers me.

If you have children at home and your response is that you work, particularly full time, the next question will have something to do with how you manage it and who cares for the children. I translate this to mean, "You can't possibly be doing both jobs properly," or "Why aren't you doing what you're supposed to do?"

On the other hand, if you respond that you are at home raising your children, I guarantee that the next question will have something to do with your well-being, or what you do to keep your sanity. The implication of this question seems to be that anyone in the company of children for an extended period of time certainly must be losing her mind.

This is clearly a no-win situation. You have a choice between condemnation as a neglectful mother or a pea-brain — take your pick. Many women are so defensive about their work status that they anticipate the second question, and immediately explain their child care arrangements or provide a list of daily, worthwhile activities in order to justify their choices.

THE NEW AMERICAN WOMAN

The rapid societal change we have experienced has caused a division between women which is really devastating to witness. The image of the American Woman has taken a 180-degree turn in one generation. Gone are aprons, cookies, and the PTA and in are briefcases, meals out, and day care. Yet the "New American Woman" also spends quality time with her children (no more than two) and has a marvelous egalitarian relationship with her husband. Those women who have chosen to work are busy lowering actuarial mortality tables in an effort to live up to this image. Those who have chosen to be homemakers find themselves "out of it" and battling for respect.

It is not only women at home who exhibit a lack of self-esteem. Ellen Goodman comments in her book, *Turning Points,* that not only have we made it difficult for women who choose to be homemakers, but also for those who desire to pursue a traditionally "female" career such as nurse or secretary. As women discover the limitless options open to them and begin to infiltrate fields which have been dominated by men in the past, labor shortages are becoming apparent in some of these "female" occupations. "Women's work" has come to mean "inferior work." Parents encourage their daughters to become business executives and doctors, not secretaries and nurses.

If the comparable pay movement achieves any success, it will be interesting to see how much of the labor force shift is attributable to job function versus inadequate compensation. Are clericals applying to training programs for blue-collar trades because they enjoy the work or because they can make twice the money? Would teachers, librarians, and social workers be more satisfied if their compensation were equivalent to degree holders in business and engineering?

The duties and job security of homemakers are not what they used to be. Homemakers no longer "make" everything in the home, and it is not a lifelong occupation in today's society. With the rising divorce rate, a spouse's income can hardly be regarded as one's "social security" either. The changes have brought about a different job description for women at home and subsequent pressure to expand their horizons in some way outside of the home. This pressure has pushed women in two directions; either with the millions who have joined the labor force or with others who have fought back with what Goodman calls "Housewife Pride."[1] The two sides have started a war.

My own introduction to this war came shortly after my first child was born. I was working to promote the concept of part-time employment opportunities for professionals and setting up volunteer liaisons with organizations I felt would view this as a common goal, such as groups representing older workers, entrepreneurs, the handicapped, and women. The reaction from one well-known women's organization was that this was fine for clerical workers, but professionals were supposed to be "serious," i.e., work the way men always have. So much for the choices I had heard about so much.

Betty Friedan has claimed that the women's movement is evolving into a second stage, one that is more concerned about work and family issues. She claims that the attempt to ratify the Equal Rights Amendment failed, not due to issues of equality, but because of the movement's blind spot about the family. This created a polarization between women who view the family as their security and those who want to pursue different endeavors.[2]

"YEAH, BUT THEY . . ."

What kinds of things do the two sides say about and to each other? Working women claim that homemakers say or imply the following:

- Working women are selfish.
- They are cheating their children.
- They do not do their fair share of school or community activities.
- They do not reciprocate with invitations, car rides, etc.
- Their children are inferior, e.g., wild, undisciplined.
- They think their time is more important because they have jobs.
- Their jobs obviously are more important to them than their children.

Homemakers feel that working women say or imply the following:

- Homemakers do nothing all day.
- They are uninteresting.
- They have no identities of their own.
- They are constantly laying guilt trips on working mothers.
- They are reluctant to help out when working women have scheduling problems.

- They exclude nonhomemakers' children from activities.
- They are defensive.

How did this antipathy and resentment reach such a point? In a time when there were few choices, most women were doing the same thing. In one sense, it was much easier not to have to choose. Since women were all in the same situation, they had a built-in neighborhood or family support group to help share childrearing responsibilities.

As women began to have more choices and exercise them, suddenly it was a game with new rules. No one knew for certain how the game would turn out, and this made everyone a little nervous. This generation is the first to have a majority of mothers in the labor force, and a certain amount of maternal guilt and self-doubt accompany this pioneering effort. How will her children turn out? Will she regret the missed time with them? Is it worth all the juggling?

Meanwhile homemakers feel that what they do is no longer considered to be enough. They resent the low esteem in which they are held, and react defensively. They want motherhood once again to be viewed as a worthwhile job, a career. One homemaker writes in a woman's magazine:

"Since trading in my white wedgies as a hospital nurse for a pair of deck shoes as a full-time mom, snubs fall on me like acid rain. Sounds paranoid, but it's true."[3]

This writer points out quite accurately that public recognition is vital to self-esteem. She wants the same approval and respect that working women receive. She closes her article with the following pleas:

- Call her job a job.
- Mention her career when introducing her.
- Converse the same way you would with anyone who has a job.
- Ask specific questions about her work.
- Realize that money is not the root of all careers.[4]

Upset over the increasing devaluation of her role, the homemaker reacts in one of two ways. One is anger at women who have made a different choice, ostensibly rejecting hers. The other is through the glorification of motherhood by trying to portray the total woman.[5] Meanwhile she's plagued by doubts: Is she too consumed with the home? What will she do when the children leave? Does anyone appreciate her?

THE RIGHT WAY

Each side seems threatening to the other. Psychologists tell us that this feeling springs forth from the self-doubt. The rare woman who feels totally comfortable with her decision remains uninvolved. However the majority of mothers project their conflicting feelings upon those who have made the opposite choice.[6] Women, more than men, seek validation and confirmation of their actions, particularly if they are insecure in their choices. They often feel personally betrayed by friends who have made the other decision.[7]

The validation process involves both defending one's own actions while judging another's. It is important for mothers to feel they have chosen the *right* way, and of course, it doesn't make sense that all options could be right. This phenomenon was apparent in our interviews. While some of the women expressed genuine empathy for one another, more often they held a higher opinion of and more understanding for people in their own situations.

PERCEPTIONS

One of the questions asked was, "What is your opinion/perception of the mother who (a) remains at home (b) works part time (c) works full time? Give me the first image or thought that pops into your head." Below are three sets of answers including three respondents each. Read through them and see how long it takes you to figure out which choice each set represents.

SET I

First respondent
   a. "overprotective of their children and more consumed with how they are doing . . . more narrowly focused . . . more dissatisfied with their lot in life . . . bored, frustrated, bitch about their husbands a lot"
   b. "the best of both worlds . . . somewhat harried, but more balanced"
   c. "often don't see they have a choice . . . some resent it and many just don't want to be at home with their kids . . . less outside interests"

Second respondent
   a. "most are bored . . . sometimes frustrated"
   b. "happiest, better for themselves and children"
   c. "driven, possibly satisfied, but also guilty"

Third respondent

    a. "some are too lazy to get up and go to work and use their brains and others stay home because they think it's important for their children"

    b. "the happy medium . . . it gives career movement and mental stability"

    c. "some who do it solely for their careers and others because they don't have any choice financially"

SET II

First respondent

    a. "aprons and entertaining, having lots of parties for the kids . . . the perfect little house, not dust or laundry baskets"

    b. "somebody who can't make the decision to go back to work or not, they really don't know which way to go"

    c. "happier, more constructive at home, more fulfilled"

Second respondent

    a. "totally involved with their children . . . have narrow vision"

    b. "a little bit everywhere . . . neither here nor there"

    c. "have a professional desire to get ahead . . . have not poured themselves totally into their children"

Third respondent

    a. "people who love mothering and being at home; but I'm not like that"

    b. "best of both worlds idealistically . . . must put career on hold"

    c. "very difficult to do . . . if they have good child care and things are going well, they're very happy"

SET III

First respondent

    a. "have their priorities in order . . . what they want to be doing most . . . feel it is most important to be at home with their children"

    b. "do it because of the necessity for extra income"

    c. "some have to work . . . others, when I see their lifestyles, that's just what they want to do"

Second respondent

    a. "an older woman in her 40's, . . . not just being at home, doing lots of things in the community . . . active, busy, intelligent, creative people"

    b. "smart way to do it . . . can further career but still have time for things that are necessary in terms of marriage, family, community, and church"

    c. "hassled, having to give up something . . . something has to give when you work full time; if you're doing your job 100%, something is missing at home"

Third respondent
   a. "women who have worked and have a very keen career sense
      and a very keen sense of self . . . enjoy their children, but
      not necessarily the household work . . . care for child overrides
      nuisances and also suppresses and diverts career and self-
      fulfillment urges"
   b. "not so frazzled as full-timers . . . have to make choices
      constantly"
   c. "highly motivated . . . harried, short-tempered, well-dressed,
      borderline frantic"

Although I'm sure I don't need to tell you, the above groups
were:

SET I   - part-time employed mothers
SET II   - full-time employed mothers
SET III - homemakers

THE GRASS IS ALWAYS GREENER

Part of the war between women is fueled by this need to justify
and validate their choices. Another reason that there is little
empathy for the "other side" is that there is no real understanding
of how the other half lives. Often we are immersed in our own
struggles, thinking others are breezing through life. Some of
the comments I heard had an undertone of, "She's taken the
easy way out; she should try doing this all day." The image
that we criticize may be just that — an image, not real people.

Most mothers of children still at home are facing
innumerable difficulties, regardless of the choices they have
made. One primary problem is that mothers feel they need to
explain their decisions. Secondly, the inaccurate pictures we
have of each other divert the focus from the real problems that
do exist.

Working mothers often are seen leaving their homes
(escaping!) in nice clothes each morning. Little thought is given
to the effort that goes into how they got out of the door, dressed
and fed, not to mention getting children ready for the day. Many
do not even have the benefit of the money or the type of job
which allows for nice clothes.

Another misconception about working is that it is always
challenging and exciting. Few jobs are fun eight hours a day.
They call it "work" because it *is*. The work does not end at
five o'clock either. Then it is time to come home to a second
job. There is little free time, and when it does appear, it is
usually spent on children and family activities, not self.

Finally, working mothers, like their unemployed counterparts, are concerned about their children and how they develop. One of my interview questions was "What is your biggest worry about the future?" The most common answer, with no correlation to work status, was "that my children turn out alright."

Bonnie, 39, is a systems engineer at IBM. She lives in Phoenix, Arizona with her husband and two sons, ages 8 and 6. She has always worked full time, and since having her children has struggled with the problems this work commitment brings.

> "There are many times when there is too much pressure. I find myself pulled in too many directions and then I don't react well. Sometimes things are just too intense . . .
> " . . . there is not enough time to do the things you'd like to do. You feel guilty . . . most of the women I work with express a certain amount of (ambivalence about) am I doing the right thing.
> "If things get too stressful at work or if all of a sudden you have to work a lot of overtime . . . there are so many little things that can just push you over as far as keeping everything in line and reasonable . . . It may be picking up a child late or not spending the time with your children you should . . . you're just pushed."

The vision of a homemaker which was jokingly reported to me more than once was the fat, slouchy lady sitting in her favorite chair eating bon-bons and watching the soaps. Apparently when their children reach school age, they forego the sweets and get exercise-mad, because the next most common image I heard was the professional tennis player and club woman.

In reality, any woman committed to providing quality care for her children and managing a smooth household has a formidable job. The rewards are there, but the frustrations are many. They are even more evident to a generation of educated women with several years of work experience behind them.

Reasoning with a two-year old can be infinitely more difficult than discussions with even the most cantankerous boss. Lack of adult companionship is a real problem to many homemakers who find themselves in deserted neighborhoods, alone to amuse their progeny. There is very little closure to the work and some of the tasks remain the same forever. There also is no tangible compensation for the homemaker's efforts, and "career advancement" may mean moving from diapers to drugs.

Joy, 33, is a homemaker living in Rochester, Minnesota. She has three children, ages 10, 7, and 2. For sometime following the birth of her first child, she did some substitute teaching. However, she now regrets the time she spent working, and has decided that she could not be happy with any form of regular substitute child care. She found that her child needed her more than she needed to work. She wants to be available for her children and enjoys the flexibility of a home schedule versus an office routine. However, she talks of some of the daily frustrations:

> "Sometimes you feel that what you do gets undone very quickly, especially when you think about housework. I think that staying home with my children will pay dividends in the future, but I'm not sure I can always see that right away. Hopefully, I will when they're older . . . But the housework; it seems like you never get done with it.
>
> "Also there's no paycheck . . . nothing really concrete to show that there is appreciation for it (the work). Sometimes you don't feel appreciated . . . maybe you know you are, but you aren't really told often enough . . ."

STRADDLERS

Where does the part-timer fit into the picture? Does she tend to align herself with one side versus another? Or does she gingerly straddle the fence, ducking the passing bullets flying over her head? Most of the women I know who work part time suffer from a certain type of schizophrenia that comes from integrating rather well in both milieux. Practicing both of the options for part of the week tends to give them an understanding for the joys and frustrations of both choices. It also sometimes makes them a little self-righteous about how they refuse to identify with either of the stereotypes.

One term I hear constantly from part-time employed women is that they have the best of both worlds. Having a break from continual child care can make them more excited about the time they are with their children. Maintaining a career can remove worry about the future and provide another dimension to their lives. The variety seems to make them enjoy both jobs more.

On the other hand, the second most frequent term I hear from part-timers is "fragmentation." Their flexibility is a double-edged sword. They choose more informal child care arrangements and work schedules which allow them more time with their children. However, the informality and flexibility can create a scheduling nightmare.

Another problem part-time employed women face is full-time expectations. For one thing, there is less assistance on the home front when mom "is only working part time." For another, work loads on the job have a way of creeping toward full-time hours, yet too many women are unable to duplicate the level of responsibilities in a part-time job that they would assume by working full time. Some of the expectations are self-imposed by women who decide they will do it all as well as those who have clearly chosen to devote more hours to one of their commitments.

Rosanne, 31, worked part time for several years after her daughter was born. She was the director for a nonprofit childbirth organization and a conference planner for a university in the Washington, DC metropolitan area. When her second child was a few months old, she accepted a full-time position as the assistant director for development at the university. She has ambivalent feelings about her part-time career:

> "Up until this year I worked part time because of the children. I had to consider what the transition would mean to the children and the family as a whole. I was not being fulfilled career-wise when I was working part time. I could not find a line of work I was willing to make a career out of; there were just not enough options open part time.
>
> "It was also very hectic and confusing in terms of child care. My daughter, now 4, was never sure which days I was working or what time I would be picking her up. I just realized that she needed a routine very badly. . . . I'm glad I had the time to be with them, but it's a lot of work working part time."

REDIRECTING ENERGY

Clearly there are plenty of problems and challenges to go around. Regardless of the work choice a woman makes, she is subject to questions about her actions and how this decision will affect her family and her future. Acclaim, or even understanding, may be hard to find. This we all share.

Surely there must be some common goals we also can find to share. How much more productive it would be to direct our efforts toward mandated parental leave, quality day care, or some form of compensation for work done in the home instead of criticizing those who have gone down "the road not taken."

FOOTNOTES

[1]Ellen Goodman, *Turning Points* (Garden City: Doubleday & Co., Inc., 1979), p. 211.

[2]Betty Friedan, *The Second Stage* (New York, Summit Books, 1981), p. 220.

[3]Pamela Hobbs Hoffecker, "Will the Real Working Mom Please Stand Up?" *Parents* (April, 1985), 60:4, p. 154.

[4]*Ibid.*

[5]Nancy Rubin, *The New Suburban Woman* (New York: Coward, McCann and Geoghegan, 1983), p. 133.

[6]Marguerite Hoxie Sullivan, "Mom vs. Mom," *The Washington Woman* (December, 1983), 12:2, p. 23.

[7]Barbara J. Berg, "Mothers Against Mothers," *The Washington Post* (January 3, 1986), p. B5.

3.
The Big Reason

What goes into the decision-making process for women faced with the option of employment during the child-raising years? Is the choice carefully analyzed with regard to everyone's requirements — now and in the future? Or is it a reaction to what seems to be an overwhelming problem, obstacle, need or belief? In short, how do we make the big choice?

Over the years, I've asked the women in my classes to list all of the possible reasons that they might have to work or remain at home with their children. I have divided the responses here accordingly, with the majority of the answers applicable to either choice, depending upon your orientation.

REASONS TO WORK

Money

Since few homemakers are compensated monetarily, this motivation belongs solely under the employment heading. As we will see in Chapter Five, money may mean much more than its sheer purchasing power. It may represent important intangible benefits such as power, self-esteem, and independence. In most surveys, money comes out as the primary reason that women work. This is confirmed by statistics that tell us that 27 percent of working women are married to men who earn less than $10,000 per year and 41 percent have spouses who earn below $15,000 annually.[1]

Different Dimension to Life

For some women, the traditional roles of wife and mother do not provide sufficient fulfillment. They want to have a function outside the family and home. Furthermore, many homemakers suddenly find large blocks of spare time when they send their last children off to school. Energies once funneled into volunteer activities as a diversion from household responsibilities are increasingly being directed toward paid employment.

Opportunity to Use Education and Training

We are not trained formally to be parents or homemakers. Most young women today wisely are preparing themselves for some type of job in the workplace. Unless her preparation has been focused on child development or home economics, it may be difficult for a homemaker to see how her education and training is being utilized. Particularly for women who have enjoyed their careers, giving them up even temporarily may represent quite a loss.

Self-esteem

Most homemakers today will readily admit that their vocation does not do much for their self-esteem. They feel that they need to be "something else" in order to be "somebody." The cause of these feelings is a complicated one which is explored more thoroughly elsewhere in the book, but it's fair to say that a search for identity and self-esteem generally drives women from, not to, the home.

Recognition

Closely linked to self-esteem is the need for recognition of a job well done. Mother's Day comes once a year. With any paid job, there generally is more frequent feedback about the type of work you are doing. Possibly there are some tangible results of your efforts. If nothing else, you get a paycheck. Much of the homemaker's work is intangible, repetitive and subject to being "undone" very quickly. Furthermore, much of it goes unnoticed and is taken for granted. Most children become appreciative of their parents' efforts only after they have had some on-the-job training with their own offspring.

REASONS TO REMAIN HOME

Time

There are only 24 hours in a day. Working, even on a part-time basis, will consume several of those hours. Add time spent with children, social obligations, errands, household chores, volunteer commitments, etc., and it is easy to see what is lost — time for you! Removing a job from the picture frees up time.

Autonomy

While many homemakers may protest that they are at their entire family's beck and call constantly, there usually is some degree of freedom to schedule activities and work throughout the week. Many jobs do not afford such luxury. Instead, your entire day may be planned by someone else and there is usually a boss to please.

Child Care

Many women want to be the primary caregivers to their children on a daily basis. Others might prefer to work, but do not because of lack of quality substitute child care arrangements, or because the cost of providing good child care consumes much of the additional income from paid employment. There is a critical shortage of affordable, quality child care at all socio-economic levels in our country.

Health

Women with one job should suffer less fatigue and stress than those with two. In Chapter Seven, we will look at some interesting research efforts which explore who is actually physically and mentally healthier. All things being equal, the absence of paid employment should allow the homemaker to take better care of herself physically. Certainly there are many women at home, particularly those with infants and toddlers, who are under more physical stress than their employed counterparts. However, adding a paid work commitment onto innumerable others is just one more obstacle preventing a sick woman from getting to bed or from getting the rest needed to fight off illness in the first place.

Clear Priorities

By virtue of the fact that they have left jobs to remain at home with their children, homemakers clearly have made the statement that their priorities are family and home. Working women, whether or not they have a choice in the matter, must redefine priorities constantly. Sick children, snow days, school plays, etc., all call for choices. Only a very few working mothers can afford the type of substitute care that will replace them in most circumstances. Therefore, they are constantly juggling priorities, often feeling extremely fragmented.

REASONS TO DO EITHER

Precious Years

Women at home often state that the first years of a child's life are so important to how he or she grows and develops that they would not dream of turning their children over to a substitute caregiver during those precious years. It is an unfortunate fact that women's childbearing years coincide directly with the period of most rapid professional growth. These precious years in the job arena are precisely when many careers are made or broken.

Better Parent

I have heard women who have tried all of the various options claim that they are better parents because of their choices. The bottom line does not seem to be whether or not the mother works, but how satisfied she is with her work status. Happy people make happy workers, wives and mothers. Conversely, frustration and dissatisfaction rarely are contained in one area of a person's life.

Enjoyment

Not everyone is fortunate enough to be able to say they enjoy those activities which consume a large portion of each day. I have always measured job satisfaction by how quickly the day passes (if it goes too slowly, I am bored) and by whether or not I dread getting up in the morning. I am by nature a night person, so if I am reasonably lucid and pleasant in the morning, it means I am enjoying my work. Do you look forward to each day's agenda? This should be an important ingredient of your choice.

Intellectual Stimulation and Growth

A sense of being challenged and of growing is not limited to either an office or the home. Women seeking to expand their horizons can do so in any environment.

Competence

Competence comes from doing a job well. This job could be running a home or a million-dollar corporation. I also have noted that competence seems to be self-perpetuating. The satisfaction which comes from completing a task in an outstanding manner encourages people to repeat the performance in other areas. I am sure you can think of individuals who just seem to do everything well and "have it all under control."

Role Model

Many women regard the choice to work or not as being integral to the role model they want to present to both their daughters and their sons. They do not want their children necessarily to follow in their footsteps, but if the parents' behavior is mimicked by their offspring, they want it to serve them well.

Meet New People

This often is associated with getting out in the workplace. The office environment does provide another milieu in which to expand personal and professional contacts. However, in some instances the woman at home may have far more opportunities to initiate activities which put her in contact with new acquaintances than women in certain types of jobs.

The Future

Concerns about the future affect all women. Mothers who work wonder if they will look back and regret the time absent from their families. Mothers who devote themselves to home and family wonder if their efforts will be appreciated and what will occupy their time when their children leave home. It is a wise woman who makes her choice based not only on the present, but also with an eye to where she wants to be ten or twenty years from now.

Pressure from Others

Not all reasons are good ones. Many women respond to the pressures placed upon them to live up to the expectations that others hold for them. Trying to fulfill roles that others choose for you usually leads to frustration. It is hard enough to meet self-imposed goals. Trying to please other people who may have conflicting expectations may be impossible.

"SPUR-OF-THE-MOMENT" CHOICES

The way in which women make the work choice is as varied as their personalities and backgrounds. Some women actually wake up one day and by that evening, they have drastically changed their lives, seemingly with no premeditation. In actuality, there probably has been a period of dissatisfaction, and either an opportunity suddenly presents itself which leads in a new direction or circumstances provide the "straw that breaks the camel's back."

Diane, 40, of Chatham, New Jersey had been a homemaker for several years. When her two daughters entered school, she realized that she was becoming increasingly bored at home. She had never liked housework and had not acquired an interest in volunteer or community work.

One day she glanced down at a paper lying on the bed and saw an open house being advertised by a temporary employment agency in a nearby town. Diane was feeling bored that day and on the spur of the moment, she decided to drive over to see what was available. She took some tests and was surprised to see how quickly her clerical skills came back to her.

> "I went home and told my husband what I had done and he almost went through the floor. He said, 'What made you do that?' and I answered, 'I really don't know; I don't know what made me do it.' An hour later the telephone rang and it was this woman asking me if I could work the next day.
>
> "I had no clothes to wear. After being at home so long, I didn't have anything I felt was appropriate for an office. I didn't know who would take care of the girls the next day. But I said yes. I knew if I said no, that they might not call back. So I went (to work) the next day and I've been working there for five years now, six months as a temporary and then I transferred to a full-time job."

Susan, 34, of Billings, Montana worked full time for 15 years selling advertising for a local newspaper. She juggled her job and three children, ages 2 to 7. Her job gradually expanded into a 10- to 12-hour per day commitment. The pressure gradually expanded as well.

In her case, the straw that broke the camel's back happened to be some good news. One day, her daughter unexpectedly won a television set. Susan had been unavoidably detained at work very late. By the time she got home, her daughter was in tears, having waited so long to share her good news. Susan decided then and there that she could no longer devote so many hours to work, and that she needed a leave of absence to sort out the issues. While the decision was sudden, the problem certainly was not.

> "I wish there would have been a way for me to do my job in a shorter day . . . The job itself was so nice for so long until it became such a long day. I quit because it was the one thing I could change. It was the only way to change the job. The

job itself was not the problem. It was the hours. If only it could have been the same thing without taking up three-quarters of your life.

". . . Their (the company's) idea was to do it the way we need you to do it . . . We need you when we need you and we need you all the time. Either that or don't work here. The only way to change my situation was to change my job . . . I just couldn't get it all into a day."

STRONG BELIEFS

Some women have extremely strong feelings or beliefs which override other elements of the decision-making process. On an intellectual basis, they acknowledge they have a choice, but their convictions are so strong, it is clear that it would be virtually impossible for them to choose a course counter to those beliefs. They look at the options which confront them and see only one acceptable alternative. These beliefs could be rooted in religious convictions, socio-political views, or values shared by the person and those who are close to her. The convictions could also be the result of preconceived notions about women who make certain choices.

Susanna, 37, of Rochester, Minnesota is a board-certified internist. She met her husband, a fellow physician, at the Mayo Clinic where they both practiced medicine. She continued working the first year of their marriage, but then they jointly decided that she would resign her position in order to devote more attention to their marriage and community involvement.

The couple has had four children in the last five years. Susanna gave up her practice, but has done extensive volunteer work on two community projects.

"I was advised by many people not to leave the clinic. It was an ideal place to work . . . I could have stayed there. My husband and I decided that the choices we make in life will determine our value before the Lord for all of eternity. To be professionally involved is excellent and you can certainly help a number of people, but my relationship with my husband had to be more important.

". . . I knew that I could not do it all properly if I practiced full time. The demands on a physician are rather strong . . . I would be giving the best hours of my day to my patients. I'd come home at night and be tired; I wouldn't have much left to give to my husband.

"Certainly when the children came along, I knew that my first responsibility was to them. No one cares for a child the way a parent does. Your values can rarely be duplicated in some kind of day care center or even by another person . . . We had to define values and the fact that intangible things would be more important to us than tangible things."

Susanna made her choice based upon a religious conviction that as a woman, her primary responsibility was to her husband and children. The duties she felt called to in the home did not allow the option of pursuing a professional career on a full-time basis.

Laurie, 42, has had an equally strong commitment to her career. She lives in New York City and embarked upon a new career two years ago as the owner of a shop which sells antiques and newly crafted gifts and furniture. Her first career was with a major publishing house, beginning as an editor and working her way up to division vice president. In addition, she has written fourteen children's books.

Laurie's only child is now 13 years old. When she was born, Laurie never considered quitting her job, but was angry at the resistance she encountered.

"Women today having children have absolutely no idea how far we've come and what it was like 13 years ago . . . I'm not sure what kind of choice I had; it was either work full time or not at all. At the time, they (the publishers) never expected me to return to work. I was only the second woman in the history of the company to come back after her child was born. In fact, they told me not to come back.

". . . A part of me felt very rebellious. I was so angry that they didn't believe that I was committed to my career. Maybe I cut off my nose to spite my face and I said, 'Damn you all, I will be back.' And I came back full time plus.

"I'm not sure that was the best thing for me or my child, but I didn't have any other choice. The other choice was to be in the park with the mothers and I knew I didn't want that. So did I have a choice? I don't know; I guess so, as much as society allowed me, which was not a whole lot."

Laurie was committed to working and absolutely could not identify with women who did not have careers. She described her image of a homemaker as "someone who is boring, with a limited ability to make conversation, not necessarily unintelligent, but just without a whole lot to say. I find myself caught in corners with them at cocktail parties trying to be nice, but (trying to) get away from them." There was really only one acceptable choice for her, and she was forced to pursue it on the organization's terms.

VICTIMS OF CIRCUMSTANCE

Many women are unable to imagine that they have the power to make decisions to control their lives. They see themselves as victims of circumstance, and inaction or reaction determine their lifestyles. Most "victims" will insist they have no choice, regardless of whether they are homemakers or working mothers.

Unwilling homemakers generally cite the number of children they have or the unavailability of child care as reasons prohibiting them from working. Less often it may be lack of assistance available from a spouse, or frequent moves necessitated by the spouse's occupation. Not being able to find the right job or lack of flexibility in the workplace are other obstacles.

Unwilling workers point to finances as the main problem that keeps them in the work force. Others who acknowledge the freedom to drop out, for awhile at least, say that it would be impossible because of the detrimental effect upon their careers.

Truly there are women who would have to overcome incredible odds to feel that they could exercise a choice in the area of employment options. However, there are also innumerable examples of seemingly unhappy mothers who tend to perpetuate the conditions which cause their problems. Consider the woman who has bemoaned being tied down with preschoolers for years and then chooses to have another child when the youngest goes off to kindergarten. Or the one who is constantly complaining about bills but is in the process of buying yet a bigger and more expensive home.

For many, it is easier to try to convince themselves that they have been forced into their situations than to try to analyze or redirect their lives.

MAJOR REASONS

Most of the women I interviewed did feel they had a work choice. They insisted that it had been carefully analyzed, too, but their other remarks usually did not corroborate this claim. In many cases they had thought about their decisions a great deal. However, their efforts were usually concentrated solely on the present and in only one or two major components of the decision.

One question in the interviews was, "Explain the most important reason or deciding factor in the choice you have made or you feel has been forced upon you." Homemakers were the most unified in their responses. Without exception, their answers revolved around wanting to be with their children or wanting to be the primary influence upon their children's development.

They were unwilling to allow someone else to perform this job.

Gaylene, 30, is a homemaker in Colton, South Dakota. Her husband is an airline pilot and they have three small children. They jointly agreed upon her role as a full-time mother and Gaylene said that only real economic hardship would drive her back to the workplace.

> "My decision was made because I want to be there with the kids . . . I would dread it if I had to work and couldn't be there with them.
>
> "It's my responsibility. I shouldn't have kids and then let somebody else raise them. Also, I enjoy them, their smiles, and their imaginations. I want to see them take their first steps or see their reactions when we go to the zoo. I'm basically a child within myself and I like to enjoy those things, too. I had kids to enjoy them, not to let someone else enjoy them."

Women who work full time fell into two categories, those with older children and those with preschoolers. Mothers of older children who reentered the labor force after a stint as homemakers stated that their major reasons for working were boredom or the fact that no one needed them at home anymore. Money was only a secondary bonus. There was a further distinction between mothers of preschoolers who held professional and nonprofessional jobs. Women in nonprofessional jobs were working for the money. Those in professional jobs spoke of careers.

Marianne, 31, was on maternity leave when we spoke. Her child care arrangements had just fallen through. She could not get a visa approved for a relative of her husband's who had agreed to come from India to watch the new baby. Despite experiencing her first taste of working mothers' dilemmas, she was determined to return to her full-time job as an analyst with a New York insurance company.

> "My decision obviously had to take into account a lot of conflicting needs. It's hard to determine what the outcome will be. There's been a lack of modeling available for me.
>
> "When it came down to it, I had to decide what was best for me. This was the best thing for me to do professionally. And if my mental outlook is good, then it will be best for him" (her son).
>
> " . . . I think he will be better off with a mother who has more interests, who has not poured herself totally into her kids and who will not suffer from empty nest syndrome when he leaves."

Part-timers were the most diverse in their answers. Some were working solely for financial reasons. Others cited many of the various components listed at the beginning of the chapter, such as self-esteem, adding a different dimension to their lives, more time, etc. One common thread to the responses was the need to seek a balance between family and job-related goals.

Kathe, 37, is a self-employed accountant in Ann Arbor, Michigan. She has three children, ages 8, 6, and 3. She has tried a variety of part-time arrangements, working for herself as well as for an accounting firm. She has tried the self-employment option in her home and in an office.

> "I've made a variety of choices, always though considering how I wanted to do things. The revisions I've made, I feel like I've fine-tuned it over the years . . . to get my practice to be more of the kind of work that I wanted to do and at the same time keep my flexibility. The flexibility has always been a priority, so that I could be available to my kids, to be able to do things with them in the schools.
>
> "I think I've kept working in some ways expressly because I wanted to keep the long-term option of being able to continue that career. So I've just modified it from time to time to figure out how to make it work best in the current situation, keeping in mind that long term, I always wanted to be able to work."

DECISION PHOBIA

Linda Gray Sexton, in her book *Between Two Worlds,* tells the true stories of some "Baby Boom" women she interviewed extensively. While the issues varied, the women shared a difficulty in making decisions in many critical areas of their lives, e.g., marriage, career, parenting. She takes a sociological stab at explaining the paradox of multiple options:

We baby boomers grew up with material things which we took for granted. We didn't learn how to make choices and set priorities because we were given so much. Having more choices than our parents, but fewer skills to be able to wisely discern between them, provoked a crisis. The result was a lot of young people reaching the legal age of maturity with little idea of what they wanted, much less knowing how to get it.

Women in particular suffered from the full array of choices. Feminism exacerbated the problem by telling women not to worry about choices; they could do everything. In an age of increasing freedoms, women were not bound by traditional social mores. On the other hand, there were no role models available to look to for guidance. Sexton describes these women, this generation now facing parenting choices as "on their own, with an open sea of choice, caught between two worlds."[2]

A BETTER WAY

Most mothers I speak with express some degree of anxiety about their work choices. We have seen the reasons for this. More choices make the decision more difficult. We do not know how our children, or for that matter, how we will turn out. Will we be neurotic, narcissistic women with aimless children unable to form permanent attachments? Or will we turn out to be more balanced and happier than our parents? The uncertainty creates division and destroys the support we should be sharing.

There are two exceptions to questioning mothers. First are those individuals whose paths are dictated by conditions of their existence, voluntary or involuntary. In this category fall low-income, single parents and women with large numbers of preschool children. The second category are women who have such strong beliefs that they perceive their decision as *the only* right way. In both instances, there is no real choice seen and therefore no doubt about the route they have taken.

The rest of us, a majority, just choose to act or react. Most people react to either an immediate problem or a general sense of dissatisfaction. When they do so, they tend to focus on one area of a very complex situation. If we seek to initiate a choice with such obvious far-reaching effects, the only way to have a sense of peace about it is to thoroughly examine *all* the components of our thinking. That is what we will try to do in the next few chapters.

FOOTNOTES

[1]U.S. Department of Labor, Bureau of Labor Statistics. "Employment in Perspective: Women in the Labor Force." Report 725, Washington, DC, 1985.

[2]Linda Gray Sexton, *Between Two Worlds* (New York, NY: William Morrow & Co., Inc., 1979), p. 29.

4.
The Big Equation

It always helps me to write things down on paper. Then I can stare at all of the components of an issue in one spot. The answer may not leap at me off of the page, but I feel as though I have contained the factors and have more control over evaluating them.

Therefore, I suggest that you write a "big equation" to help you make your big choice. This will not be an equation that can be solved in numbers. Furthermore, it will be different for each person. There will be an answer, but the answer may change over time. It would be nice to get the "right" answer that would serve us for all time, but life does not offer such certainties.

Actually the equation starts off very simply:

$$\text{FINANCES} \pm \text{SELF} \pm \text{CHILD} \pm \text{OTHERS} \pm \text{SOCIETY} = \text{WORK OPTION}$$

Most of the components of your decision will fall into one of five major areas:

- The constraint imposed or freedom allowed by your family's financial situation.
- Your feelings and desires regarding employment and the effects this decision will have upon you now and in the future.
- What is best for your child.
- The input and the amount of support you can expect from others.
- The degree to which society facilitates your choice.

From analyzing these components, you can come up with an answer or a work option which best meets your needs.

WORK OPTIONS

Let's start at the end. Unlike some mathematical equations where there may be an infinite number of choices as answers, this one has a limited amount of options. The choices you have regarding work are:

- Unemployment
- Permanent part-time employment
- Full-time employment
- Free-lance and consulting work
- Owning your own business
- Taking a leave of absence from your job

There are some general observations that can be made about these various work patterns. However, the choice of any of these options for you will depend upon many factors: your work history, the amount of risk you feel comfortable taking, the age of your children, your personality, your long-term goals, and others.

UNEMPLOYMENT

Homemakers often are described as women who do not work. There is no such thing as a homemaker who does not work. We usually omit the end of the phrase "for money." Most homemakers are not paid for their services. However, there is currently a move in Congress to provide some of the same types of benefits to homemakers which have been afforded to employed individuals, such as retirement and various types of insurance. For statistical purposes, homemakers have always been considered to be unemployed.

There is a second phrase used commonly by me as well as many of the women in this book for which I feel I should apologize. I have learned that homemakers do not like to be referred to as "women who stay at home." While this would seem like a wonderful luxury to me on certain hectic weeks, apparently it carries a connotation of "doing nothing." We can all probably think of homemakers who are so involved in community, personal, or children's activities that they are home no more than employed women. The reference to "women at home" throughout this book is really a synonym for homemakers, and carries no pejorative implications.

The primary reason that most younger women choose to be homemakers is to care for their children. In general, homemakers have more time with their children because a paid job does not demand their attention. Choosing to withdraw from the labor force will have an obvious negative impact upon lifetime earnings and possible negative consequences for future career status.

Statistics show us that the number of homemakers is dwindling. In 1986, only 37 percent of mothers with children under 18 were not in the labor force.[1] Most of us do not need statistics to be aware of that fact. When I was growing up, I had only one friend with a working mother and she had not taken a job until her daughter became a teenager. In contrast, there is only one homemaker within a two-block radius of my house today. I vividly remember taking my daughter for walks in her stroller and having the odd sensation of going through a ghost town in the Old West.

Heather, 41, of Washington, DC, had worked as a personnel administrator before giving birth to her first child at age 39. She is now a homemaker who also has a minor time commitment to a small family business. Because she had already experienced many years of employment, Heather's appraisal of her current status centered primarily around her relationship with her son. She did not appear as concerned about her future work life as many younger mothers seem to be:

> "The advantages of being home are legion. Because I'm there virtually all the time with my child, I don't miss the stages, or little things, that both mothers and fathers kind of mourn — because they do pass very quickly. I can turn on a recording device and screen phone calls so I have an option of whether I want to let a call go or catch it right away. I'm able to keep up generally with household work. I'm able to schedule my day much more under my control — when I do my errands, when I have people come to do repairs, when I get to the Post Office, etc.
>
> "I think the major disadvantage is that with a child as young as mine (15 months), he needs a lot of personal attention. He's very easily distracted and I'm his prime distraction. I don't usually get to complete anything; I end up going back to virtually everything. I was frustrated by that for a time and there are still days that I feel frustrated by it, but most of the time I'm just enjoying rocking along with him."

PERMANENT PART-TIME EMPLOYMENT

Part-time employment would seem to be the logical preference for mothers, particularly those of preschoolers. You can maintain a career and still have time to spend with your children. The money is not as good as working full time, but better than nothing. Your career probably is in a holding pattern, but still there.

As women poured into the work force in the 1970s, part-time employment grew twice as fast as full-time employment. By the early 1980s, one out of five people worked part time, four-fifths of them by choice. Approximately two-thirds of part-timers are women.

Of mothers with children under sixteen, 27 percent work less than thirty-five hours per week. One-third of working mothers with preschool children work part time.[2] The figures would be higher if there were a larger number of good part-time jobs available and if women had the option of reducing hours on jobs they had held on a full-time basis prior to becoming mothers.

For years, part-time employment was synonymous with low-paying, dead-end jobs. Indeed the average wage of a part-timer still is one-half the hourly rate a full-timer receives.[3] However, in recent years there has been a movement to expand and upgrade the status of part-time employment. More than two million professionals now hold part-time jobs.[4]

Neva, 29, of Silver Spring, Maryland, works as an analyst for a local government. She has a job-shared position which was created at her request after the birth of her second son eight months ago. Her work schedule is 20 hours per week. She receives one-half of her former salary, full health insurance, and the remainder of her employee benefits are prorated.

Neva also has a two-and-a-half year old son. Looking back over her past decisions, she states that she regrets not working part time earlier. Of her current situation, she says:

"Working part time allows me time to spend with the kids, which I think for my older one is very important because he's really at an age where his mind is going crazy. Every day he comes up with new lines. I think it's very important that he gets to spend more than one hour in the evenings and weekends with me. Before we only had an hour to an hour and a half together on weekdays and that was 'fussy hour' so it's certainly not quality time. (Working part time) allows me time to cook and I find that I'm much more relaxed. It's not only improving my marital situation, but it's making me much more productive at work. I probably put out 70 percent working half-time of what I did when I was full time.

"The disadvantage is obviously that the paycheck and leave accumulation is half the size. I don't think you can make a whole lot of money working part time. Even in a well-paying job you have so many expenses working. I think most women who work part time do so for career movement and mental stability. For me, it's a happy medium."

FULL-TIME EMPLOYMENT

Most mothers who work are still doing it the nine-to-five way. In general, they will advance faster professionally and make more money on an hourly basis than they would holding an identical job at reduced hours. Most mothers who are employed full time have not managed to retire from their other unpaid job at home. This makes for a long workday. Full-time employed mothers most likely will not feel that they have enough time with their families. Personal pursuits and leisure are next to impossible to schedule.

Government numbers inform us that many women clearly work out of economic need. One out of four mothers in the labor force is maintaining a family. The number of female-headed households has more than doubled in the last twenty years with 69 percent of these mothers with children under 18 in the labor force. Their median annual income in 1983 was $13,609 and 50 percent of their jobs are in the clerical and service categories.[5]

It is not only the single parents who are struggling financially. Despite all the publicity given to consumer-crazy, self-indulgent yuppies, most of the "Baby Boom" generation will not live as well as their parents did. A study commissioned by the Joint Economic Committee reports that middle-class people between twenty and forty years old have experienced a dramatic decline in ability to achieve financial security. Fewer than half own their own homes, and male wage-earners had slower income growth than their fathers. Those who do manage to grab hold of "the good life" usually have two spouses working and fewer children.[6]

Diane, 40, of Chatham, New Jersey, was a homemaker for ten years before returning to work full time as a clerk for a natural gas company (introduced on p. 38). Her income has made it possible for her family to keep up in an affluent suburb. Her mother lives with her and helps care for two teenage daughters. Diane enjoys her job and feels more fulfilled working than she did as a homemaker.

"There are many financial advantages of my job. I also think it's been very good for me — it's made me feel better about myself and it's been very good for my marriage. I think my husband looks at me somewhat differently . . . he respects me more. Everything we do now is more of a joint effort. Before it was like I almost felt guilty for getting the one little thing I liked or doing what I wanted to do.

"Of course, there are times I can't be with the girls — to go to school functions and class trips. Not being able to do things with neighbors or friends or family . . . socializing. Working full time limits you; you only have so many weeks vacation a year. You can't just go and do as much as you would like to. The advantages for me (of working full time) have far outweighed any disadvantages.''

Some women who work full time deal with the problem of lack of time with their children by arranging their hours in a nontraditional way. A compressed workweek packs longer hours into fewer days; the most common form being the four-day, ten-hour week. If you do not have a couple of hours of commuting time tacked on to the day, this may be a good alternative for you. One "free" day can do an enormous amount for your sanity.

Another option that many workers in this country are enjoying is flexitime. There's usually a core period in the middle of the day when you must work. However, there may be a two- or three-hour range of starting and quitting times. Flexitime can help parents get children off to school in the morning or allow them to be home in the afternoon. It might help you to avoid rush-hour traffic, too!

Unfortunately, there are not sufficient firms offering flexible working hours to meet the demand of workers seeking them. While most experimental programs have been successful, many employers fear giving up too much control or possible abuse of scheduling freedom. Hence, most full-time employees are forced to function within rigid time frames. Children, babysitters, medical appointments, school activities, and illness do not always respect these schedules. Parents are forced to choose between work and conflicting needs when some flexibility in workhours would eliminate the conflict.

Some members opt for shift work. Jane, 30, lives in a small town of 100 people in Nebraska. Her two children are 8 and 4 years old. The family lives on a farm where they raise hogs. Her husband also works as a welder at a woodburning stove factory.

Faced with mounting debts, Jane increased her hours to full time last year. She is employed as a dispatcher for the local police and is on the 11:00 p.m. to 7:00 a.m. shift. She talks about the pros and cons of shift work:

"By working nights, I'm here every day when my son comes home from school and I have all my evenings free so I can go to school activities. I can sleep while my little girl is in preschool. So the sleep pattern really is pretty good.

"The disadvantage is the fact that I don't sleep with my husband but two nights a week and I don't have weekends free.

We don't have a long period of time where we can do anything together. And the job certainly still cuts down on the time I have with my kids and with my family and friends. I miss that a lot. I don't have the time that I'd like to do crafts and keep the house up. But of course, there's the money."

FREE-LANCE AND CONSULTING WORK

A free-lancer or consultant works with no permanent contractual commitment to an employer. You agree to work for a specified duration or on a particular project, usually for an hourly or daily rate with no fringe benefits. You may have an agreement or contract with several employers or clients simultaneously. Free-lance or consulting work sometimes is conducted within the framework of a small business.

Free-lance work can be performed at all different skill levels. Services which are commonly offered on a free-lance basis include writing, editing, abstracting, indexing, photography, research, accounting, bookkeeping, secretarial, child care, word processing, teaching, training, cleaning, fundraising, and computer programming. Your services are for hire and each assignment or job is negotiated with the employer.

A special type of free-lancing is temporary work through an agency. The temporary employment service acts as a middleman to match willing workers to needy businesses. An estimated 600,000 people do temporary work daily, making the industry second in size only to government. Over 90 percent of American businesses use temporary help on a regular basis.[8]

As a temporary, you maintain some control over when and where you work, but forego the pluses and minuses of self-employment. If you do not possess a list of eager clients, a temporary employment agency will provide the needed work as well as some valuable experience and contacts.

Temporaries were once synonymous with clericals, but recently there has been expansion into other fields, such as health care, data processing, light industry, and professional and technical services. The explosive growth in the temporary help industry has created fierce competition among agencies. This has resulted in better benefits to temporaries, including insurance, paid vacations and holidays, merit pay increases, profit sharing, and training programs.

There are all sorts of consulting possibilities for women with expertise in various fields. Consultants are distinguished from free-lancers in that they usually work for clients in a client-directed environment. Consultants rarely work without a contract, whereas free-lancers frequently market a finished product or service. Consultants are more likely to operate within the confines of a small business.

Consultants may be specialists with expertise to sell, or they may be generalists who assist firms with managerial functions. Some of the more common areas in which consulting contracts are awarded are training, feasibility studies, procurement, testing, survey research, planning, recruitment, operations, public relations, and marketing. Actually, consulting is a viable option any time there is an organization with a problem or need which can't be handled internally due to time constraints or lack of appropriate personnel.

Opportunities are increasing for free-lancers and consultants, because employers are aware of both the costs and risks of permanent employees. Salaries and fringe benefits are an expensive budget item if the employee is not being utilized 100 percent of the time. Furthermore, in our litigious society, employers are fearful of hiring a "bad apple" who may prove next to impossible to fire. Thus, the option of hiring someone to do a specific job with clearly defined time and monetary limitations becomes increasingly attractive to employers.

As a free-lancer or consultant, you generally have more control over your working hours than someone who has a permanent job. The flexibility and the variety of assignments are the two reasons many people choose this work option. In addition, if you're successful, you can make a lot of money.

The main drawback to free-lancing is its unpredictability. There may be times when there is no work (and no money) and times when you have several big projects due simultaneously. Some types of free-lance or consulting work require extensive time and research in preparing proposals for contracts. The preparation may be in vain if your proposal is not selected.

Suzie, 37, left her job as a teacher several years before her children, now 6 and 3 years old, were born. Although she sometimes regrets having been so consumed with home and family life, most of her memories as a homemaker are happy ones. She lives in Herndon, Virginia.

Two years ago Suzie's husband decided to leave the family. She has been able to stay in her house because he gives her voluntary child support payments in excess of what a court would order. Still, money is a scarce commodity. It was evident to Suzie that a full-time job would be the best solution for her financially and professionally. However, she felt her younger son would be adversely affected in the care of a babysitter full time. Suzie has opted to substitute teach, and provide child care for friends and neighbors. She has no regular schedule and works when she is called if it is feasible for her. Of her unpredictable arrangements, she says,

> "I need to supplement the money he (her husband) is giving us. The babysitting enables me to stay home with the children a little bit more and not have to go out. The advantage of substituting is that I can adjust my schedule according to when I want to go in and where I want to go. I have the flexibility to say 'Yes, I'll come in today' or 'No, I'll stay home.'
>
> "The primary disadvantage is getting babysitting for my children. It's something I really struggle with – not wanting to leave the children and not having permanent arrangements. It's hard always having to call to make arrangements. There are often tears in the morning from the kids — 'Do I have to get up?' 'Do I have to go to that babysitter?' It's just a struggle in the morning."

OWNING YOUR OWN BUSINESS

Owning your own business means a high degree of control and total responsibility. The time commitment can range from a few hours a month to eighty hours per week. There may or may not be some control over your workload.

In 1985, 2.8 million, or nearly six percent of all employed women were working for themselves. The majority (55 percent) were 25 to 44 years old. Women now comprise 30 percent of all self-employed workers.[8] One-half of the self-employed women are in the retail trade or personal services businesses. There has been a rise in recent years of women who operate business services, such as advertising and social service industries.

Some women choose to start a business because it will mesh more easily with their parenting roles. A larger percentage of self-employed women work part time. The part-time rate for all women is 33 percent and for the self-employed, it climbs to 44 percent. At the other end of the scale, however, the self-employed exceed the rest of the female labor force in hours worked. Approximately 16 percent of women work more than 40 hours per week; 30 percent of self-employed women work in excess of 40 hours.[9]

There are many motivations for those who decide to start small businesses. Being your own boss allows you not only to set your working hours, but to define what you do while you work. You can test your creativity, expand your areas of competence, and see your idea to completion. All of the profits from your efforts are yours.

On the other hand, the losses all belong to you, too. Job security is questionable. According to the Small Business

Administration (SBA), most new businesses will not survive past five years. The main reasons for small business failure are poor management and an inability to anticipate cash requirements.

If you hope to make a substantial profit from your business venture, you should not proceed without the advice of professionals. An accountant can set up your books and provide guidance on income taxes, investments and financing. A good insurance agent will analyze what type of coverage you need. An attorney may be necessary to review contracts and to help you avoid or survive litigation. The paper work for small businesses is incredible. There may be permits, licenses, and taxes for various government jurisdictions.

Laura, 30, resides in Salt Lake City, Utah. When the first of her three children was born six years ago, she had a teaching contract. Although the second income would have made her family financially comfortable, Laura's Mormon upbringing had impressed upon her that she would be a mother first and a teacher second. She started a tutoring business by going to parents of children having academic problems. Initially she scheduled her appointments when her baby was sleeping or in the evenings when her husband was available to be with their child. Soon the business mushroomed.

As her family expanded, Laura added a new small business — she started a preschool. The school was in her home for several years before she moved it to another location. Running a business has helped her provide extra income for the family without being apart from her children.

"The best thing about my business is that I have my children with me. Secondly, I'm my own boss. I can pretty much control what I need to do. If my kids are sick, then I can make other arrangements. Also I have to admit to another advantage — it does help my ego. I enjoy still having my hand in the pie. Finally it provides money for our family so that we are able to get out of debt and start working toward goals of things that we would need and want for ourselves and for our children.

"The problems right now are that originally when I started the preschool I had it in my own home so that I didn't have to bundle up kids to take them where I went. Now it is no longer in my own home and it is a chore to get everybody up, ready, cleaned up, and out the door, particularly in bad weather. It's also a disadvantage as far as having to live a very structured lifestyle. My kids have to be used to 'this is when we do things,' every day is the same. We all have commitments we need to make."

WORKING AT HOME

Women who free-lance, consult, or own a small business often work at home. The Chamber of Commerce of the United States estimates that 10 million businesses are run from home. Less frequently, individuals are employed by organizations with the understanding that home also will serve as office. Futurists predict that telecommuting will become commonplace as the computer becomes our main method of business communication.

Combining home and office has its own special set of benefits and drawbacks. A home office will reduce or eliminate the amount of child care you need. Rush-hour traffic, parking problems, and commuting expenses are also waived. You do not need a magnificent wardrobe and you can take a break and exercise or catch your favorite television show if the mood strikes. You escape the games and politics of the office setting.

The obvious problem is that it becomes difficult to separate your two roles. You can not leave the office or the children. Interruptions and distractions are increased. Many people do not respect your work time; if you are home, you are not regarded as really working. Some women may miss the contact with other adults, and the professional stimulation from business colleagues. Others may find their professional lives challenged when a screaming baby suddenly interrupts an important business call. Many respond that it is easier to become a workaholic when the work is always there and that family squabbles increase in the close quarters.

I worked at home for three years. I am not sure I would do it differently if I had another chance. My children did not spend an entire day at a babysitter's house until they were 4 years and 18 months old, and then it was only one day a week. Those are years that I did not want to miss being there for them. However, it certainly was not easy.

I had a telephone answering machine and used it frequently. Nevertheless, that little red light indicating a message had been received haunted me until I returned the call. The nature of my job at the time meant that the phone rang day and night. I am much happier now not seeing the messages until I am back in the office.

My most vivid memories of those years are rushing to get something accomplished in my few moments of peace. Too often, naptime stories and songs were hastily performed before dashing to return phone calls in that precious hour of quiet. I spent many days feeling quite fragmented. Of course, these problems are greatly diminished for mothers of school-aged children.

LEAVE OF ABSENCE

Most leaves of absence are taken immediately after the child is born. Maternity policies differ in each organization. Congress passed the Pregnancy Disability Act in 1978 which mandates that employers treat pregnancy and childbirth as any other temporary disability. Some firms provide a paid maternity leave and others require the employee to use accumulated sick or vacation leave. The average time a woman remains off work after the birth of a child is six weeks to three months.

Occasionally, women are able to get a leave of absence for nonmaternity reasons. Unfortunately, it may come as a result of some personal crisis. Some women are taking leaves of absence to sort out how they feel about the big choice.

Susan, 34, is a mother of three children ages seven and under in Billings, Montana (introduced on p. 38). She had worked full time for 15 years for the same organization selling advertising. Her job required many ten- to twelve-hour days. Eventually the pressure got to her and she took a leave of absence several months ago to see how she would fare staying at home. Recently, she resigned from her position.

> "It took me a long time to decide what I wanted to do and that's why I took a leave of absence. I needed to see if it was the job or a combination of a lot of things that was getting to me. The job itself had definitely gotten overwhelming and along with everything at home it was just too much for me.
>
> "My children hadn't really started to suffer as far as grades or anything, but I didn't see any point in pushing it any further . . . I wasn't enjoying life anymore, I was just rushing through it."

A leave of absence may be an excellent choice for a mother who needs time to think through the issue or one who wants a trial run as a homemaker.

THE OTHER HALF OF THE EQUATION

Those are your options. Throughout the next several chapters, we will evaluate the five main components of the big choice. We will explore some extrinsic factors of money as well as a financial analysis of the two-income family. Your well-being will be treated in terms of professional and personal considerations.

Next we will review existing research concerning the effects of maternal employment on the child and consider which type of care is best for your unique son or daughter. The other influential people in your life who will be considered are spouse, relatives, friends, and neighbors. Finally, we will look at the degree to which society affects your choice.

So now our equation looks like this:

FINANCES	±	SELF	±	CHILD	±	OTHERS	±	SOCIETY	=	WORK OPTIONS
Extrinsic Factors		Professional		Research Findings		Husband		Expectations		Unemployment
Income Worksheet		Personal		Needs of your child		Relatives		Supports		Part-time Employment
						Friends				Full-time Employment
						Neighbors				Free-lance and Consulting Work
										Own business
										Leave of absence

YOUR ANSWER

Make an equation for yourself and fill it in with any points which are relevant to your decision. There may be some issues that are of no importance to you. On the other hand, you may have some unique circumstances in your life which are not covered in this book. You may list something as a "plus" that another woman would rate a "minus."

Not only will this equation be unique for each woman, but if you were to redo it one year from now, it undoubtedly would change. A mother of a teenager may have very different concerns than a mother of an infant. Circumstances, particularly unexpected ones, may alter your equation dramatically.

Finally, to make your task even more difficult, you must consider the effects of your choice upon your future as well as its impact upon your current situation. That's one of the reasons the big choice is so complex — what is best for today may not be best for tomorrow.

When you have completed the book and your equation, share it with family, friends and/or acquaintances for some feedback. Their comments may validate your choice or may make you think twice.

Once, when I had a difficult professional decision to make, I wrote down all the pros and cons and called a half-dozen friends to ask their advice. They unanimously voted for a certain choice, the opposite of what my husband advised! My choice ended up coinciding with my spouse's, and years later I look back believing it was right. However, my friends' comments were extremely helpful in evaluating the situation objectively.

So, grab a pen or pencil if you haven't done so already and plot out your big choice!

FOOTNOTES

[1]National Commission on Working Women, "Child Care Fact Sheet," (1986), p. 1.

[2]"Working Mothers Reach Record Number in 1984," *Monthly Labor Review* (December, 1984), 107:12, p. 32.

[3]*Part-Time Employment in America* (Washington, DC: Association of Part-Time Professionals, 1985), p. 13.

[4]Diane S. Rothberg and Barbara Ensor Cook, *Part-Time Professional* (Washington, DC: Acropolis Books, 1985), p. 13.

[5]Bureau of Labor Statistics, United States Department of Labor, "Employment in Perspective: Women in the Labor Force," Report 7300, p. 1.

[6]Jane Seaberry, "Baby Boomers Find Tough Financial Sledding," *The Washington Post* (December 8, 1985), p. A2.

[7]Demaris C. Smith, *Temporary Employment* (White Hall, VA: Betterway Publications, Inc., 1985), pp. 107–108.

[8]Bureau of Labor Statistics, United States Department of Labor, "Employment in Perspective: Women in the Labor Force," Report 725, 1985, p. 1.

[9]*Ibid.*, p. 1.

5.
Money, Money, Money

Ask most people why they work and the response will be, "Money." It may be the easy, obvious answer, but not necessarily an accurate or honest one. In probing peoples' responses, the true motivation for working often has nothing to do with money, or it is a tangential factor to money, such as self-esteem, independence, or power.

The importance of money in the decision to work cannot be ignored. For many of the women we interviewed, their employment was indeed necessary to keep a "roof over their heads and food on the table." In fact, for most of the country's single parents and the 41 percent of working women who are married to men earning less than $15,000 per year, employment undoubtedly is not viewed as a choice. For others, a second income means the difference between making ends meet and having money for the "extras."

Joleen, 38, is a full-time working mother from Annandale, Virginia. She has two teenagers and has worked since the younger child was 18 months old in a variety of secretarial and office manager positions. Currently, she is an administrative assistant at a trade association.

When her children were younger, Joleen worked because it was financially necessary. Her husband decided to attend law school after several years in the armed forces. As his income rose, Joleen found that more of the money she made could go for "the fun things."

"We enjoy traveling and vacations and we have children who enjoy these things with us. We take ski trips a lot.

"Rick and I both enjoy the fact that if we need something, for instance, clothes, we don't have to budget in every single item. If we really want to do something, we can. We just bought

Shelly (her 16-year-old daughter) a car for Christmas. We'd never be able to do that without my salary.

"Another extra is a Catch-22. We eat out more often which is both because of time and ease. It's definitely more fun to work for these things than to keep the lights on in the house. It's more fun, but more controversial. When you don't have a choice, you do it and you don't have to justify it or deal with the guilt. When you do have a choice, there are a lot more considerations."

Finally, there are families for whom almost no amount of additional income would make much difference because each increase in earnings would be followed automatically by an equivalent increase in spending. Many people tend to live to the level of income they have, regardless of what it is. There is always a bigger house, a faster car, a nicer wardrobe, or another trip.

Our interviews confirmed this phenomenon. One question asked was, "How much more money (gross) per year would be necessary to your family income so that money absolutely would not be a consideration in your choice?" The responses ranged from nothing to $100,000. However, most of the answers fell into the $15,000 to $25,000 range, just enough to raise the standard of living to the next level.

SELF-ESTEEM

What money can *buy* is often not as important as what it *represents*. A paycheck shows that someone thinks you are worthwhile enough to pay you for your work; it all too graphically illustrates exactly what value you have to your employer on a hourly, weekly, or monthly basis. It's not surprising that many women arrive at a minimum salary requirement for not only what it will buy, but for what it says about them.

Alice, 32, is a homemaker who has followed her husband up and down the East Coast as he has climbed the corporate ladder of a major oil company. She has two children and a Masters degree in Nursing. She freely admits that she does not need to work for financial reasons. Alice enjoys being at home and the opportunity it gives her to pursue personal interests, be an active participant in her children's daily lives, and volunteer in community activities. As her children get older (now 10 and 7), Alice has looked into a couple of part-time employment opportunities.

In evaluating prospective salaries, she states:

"I'm working backwards. I'm delighted with our income

and see it doing nothing but going up. I'm delighted with some of the opportunities it has provided us. Yes, I'd like to be filthy rich like everyone would, I guess. But in terms of realistic goals, when and if I choose the manner of employment I want for myself, I know that my own personal worth is such that I don't want to be paid peanuts. That's a consideration. I don't have the pressure or drive though to eliminate those jobs that may be fascinating but don't have the income to go along with it.

"I would want some kind of income to make worth the time I'd be putting in. I'm not sure what the number is. A couple of years ago I looked into a position as director of a day care center. The bottom line for all the time I would be spending there plus doing the books — a whole life — was $14,000. Well, I just wasn't ready to trade off that much time for that money."

INDEPENDENCE

Money not only confers worth, it provides independence. For years, critics of the women's movement have pointed to the rising divorce rate as proof of the damage working women are doing to the family and the institution of marriage. Feminists are quick to retort that these marriages were probably bad all along and that finally women have the means to escape from them.

Today, most women spend at least several years working as adults, both before and after marriage. As we saw in Chapter One, this is a derivation from the last two generations. In the first part of this century, perhaps the era in which many of our grandparents were raised, women "of class" did not work outside the home. Even many of our mothers may have considered it unseemly for married women to work, an apparent indication that the man of the house was unable to provide for his family. An exception to this sentiment was the encouragement for women to work and support their men and their country during World War II.

Few women of this generation would even consider leaving a job simply because of marriage. The big choice comes along with the first baby. For women who have been in control of their own finances for several years, it can be quite an adjustment to suddenly need to ask for money to buy a dress, or worse yet, presents for their husbands. They feel as though they have been transported back to adolescence when they were financially dependent upon their parents and possibly managed a small allowance.

Kathleen, 39, lives in Washington, DC and has a 8-year-old daughter. She stayed at home for many years, earning an MBA in Finance in her free time. This year she reentered the labor force, working part time as a bookkeeper for two organizations. Her hours are flexible, which enables her daughter to be mostly unaffected by her mother's employment. Kathleen still juggles the many volunteer commitments that have been an important part of her life.

Kathleen could not even name a figure that would remove money as an ingredient in her decision-making process. The issue was clearly independence, not the purchasing power of her paycheck:

> "I had wanted to return to part-time work to earn my own money; I don't like being on the dole so to speak. I think my husband could be a millionaire and I would still have some of my same feelings about money. I have to have my little piddling income that I can say I produced and that I can feel that no one is looking over my shoulder at how I am spending my money."

POWER

Power and money are often companions. This might be expressed by women in terms of the influence they wield in making family decisions. Most people would concur that earning money gives that individual the right to have a voice in how it is spent. However, the issue appears to be much broader than making financial decisions. Money often is viewed as a measure of the equality of the partnership.

Some women who do not bring home hefty paychecks feel that they should defer to the major breadwinner in any matter of importance. Conversely, if the husband is important enough to earn so much money, he should not be bothered with trivial matters such as cooking, cleaning, errands and doctors' appointments. Wives who earn salaries roughly equivalent to their husbands' are likely to feel that both their time and opinions are equally valuable.

A sudden change in income in either direction for a woman may have quite an impact on her family's perception of her. Rosanne, 31, worked part time at various jobs after her children were born (introduced on p. 31). She accepted a full-time position when her younger child was a few months old. After agonizing for a year about whether or not she should make the transition to full-time work while her children were so young, Rosanne now happily claims that she has made a wise choice. Among the benefits she describes of her new full-time work status is that her husband respects her more.

> "I think my husband, this sounds so strange, likes me better working. He's been much more attracted to me over the last

six months since I started working full time. He's very proud of me and the support is just enormous.

" . . . He's given me encouragement all along and said whatever I wanted to do was fine. But I feel it more since I've been working full time. He's glad I found a 'real' job. He never considered part-time employment to be a 'real' job. He thought it was a waste of my time and my talents.

"He also knew I was unhappy when I was not working for brief periods between jobs when I was trying to figure out what to do. I was hard on him and he was patient. Now that I'm in the 'real' world, he asks for my opinion more."

SALARY EVALUATION

The financial portion of our equation is the only part which can be solved with numbers. Unfortunately, most women never sit down to figure out how much "spendable income" they are really contributing to the family coffers. Let's look at the worksheet below and consider some of the items which help us ascertain what portion of a salary will end up as money to spend:

WHAT DO I EARN?

+ Salary
  Benefits
- Benefit Contributions
- Taxes
- Child Care
- Household Help
- Transportation
- Clothing
- Meals Out
- Miscellaneous Working and Professional Expenses

WHAT DO I *REALLY* EARN?

MEET BETTY AND JOHN

To help us through our financial analysis, we will invent a woman named Betty. Betty is an accountant who worked for a CPA firm until the first of her two children was born. For the next four years, she handled some clients from a home office, grossing about $8,000 per year with part-time, flexible hours. Her husband, John, earns $40,000 annually which has not seemed sufficient for a family of four in their high-cost suburb of Dallas, Texas.

Betty has decided to return to work for her former employer, a large CPA firm. The salary she has been offered is $20,000 per year, which she hopes will go a long way to help the family catch up on some of their bills. Let's see.

Salary and Benefits

A $20,000 salary sounds like it should be a big boost to the family's income. A very important addition to that gross salary is employer-provided benefits. The latest figures from the Chamber of Commerce of the United States show that employers are paying about 38% of payroll in indirect compensation, or employee benefits.[1] Betty will get two weeks paid vacation, nine holidays and accumulated sick leave. There were no such benefits for a self-employed accountant! The firm offers group health insurance and pays 75 percent of the family premium. John's coverage through his job is quite good, so Betty waives this benefit. She does take advantage of the group life insurance and the long term disability insurance. Betty is required to join the retirement system.

Her firm will contribute a total of $5,204 in total benefits.[2] This includes Social Security (FICA) taxes, workers' compensation, unemployment insurance, paid time off from work, life insurance and retirement. While this is not money that Betty will see immediately, it certainly has value to her. Betty will have a total of $2,798 deducted from her paycheck to pay for her portion of Social Security, life insurance, long term disability insurance and retirement.[3]

Taxes

Next we come to taxes. Betty's salary will raise the family's taxable income up two brackets, or eight percentage points. The tax bracket refers to the rate that the last dollar of taxable income is taxed, not a percentage of total income that goes to the government. John's and Betty's itemized deductions for personal exemptions, mortgage interest, medical expenses, local taxes, charitable contributions, etc., equal roughly $12,000.[4] Without Betty's earnings, their taxable income would be approximately $28,000, in the 25 percent tax bracket. Betty's salary will push their taxable income to $46,000, in the 33 percent tax bracket. Based on 1986 tables, the federal tax on the second income is $5,417.[5]

Betty's income adds $18,000, not $20,000, to the taxable

income due to the two earner tax credit adjustment. Taxes for married couples had been lower for years due to community property law which stated that one-half of the man's income belonged to the wife. In 1948, Congress passed legislation allowing married couples to split the wage earner's income. Protest from singles caused a reduction in their rates in 1969.

During the 1970s, as married women flocked to the workplace, many couples learned that for tax purposes, men and women were better off living together than married if they both worked. In 1978, a husband and wife earning $20,000 each would pay $1,816 more in taxes than two single people would.[6] That year, legislation was passed which reduced but did not eliminate the marriage penalty. Betty and John may deduct from their gross income 10 percent of the qualified earned income of the spouse with lower earnings, or $3,000, whichever is less. Therefore, Betty's taxable income is reduced $2,000 from $20,000 to $18,000.

Child Care

Child care is necessary for Amy, 4, and Jason, 1, while their parents work. They have a family day-care provider who watches Jason nine hours per day and Amy five hours a day. The cost is approximately $5,148 per year.[7] Amy's half-day preschool costs an additional $1,000 for ten months. However, Amy was attending preschool before Betty returned to work so this is not considered an additional expense in our calculations. If Betty and John were to hire a child-care provider to work in their home, they would need to pay her minimum wage, as well as the employer's portion of Social Security and unemployment taxes.

Betty and John do get a child care tax credit (not a deduction) for this expense. The credit for child and dependent care expenses is 30 percent of the expenses if your adjusted gross income is $10,000 or less. The 30 percent is reduced by one percent for each $2,000 of adjusted gross income above $10,000 until this percentage is reduced to 20 percent for incomes above $28,000. The limit on expenses is $2,400 for one child and $4,800 for two or more. Hence, Betty and John get a $960 tax credit for their expenses, reducing their taxes on Betty's income to $4,457. Nearly one-quarter of her earnings is going to the Federal Government!

Transportation

Betty must get to work each day. She drives ten miles each way including stops at the sitter's house. There is no fee to park in her company's lot. Her transportation costs to commute to work for the year are $1,050.[8]

Clothing

Clothes which are suitable for an office environment do not always coincide with the wardrobe one dons to burp a baby or change a diaper. After staying at home for four years, Betty finds her clothes to be inadequate for her full-time job schedule. She spends $500 to put together a few outfits that she feels are appropriate for working in an office.

Meals Out

Betty packs her lunch a couple of days each week. She eats her noon meal in a nearby cafeteria once or twice a week. On Fridays, she goes with some colleagues for a big splurge at a favorite Italian restaurant. Once a week, Betty and John take the children to a fast food spot for a break from "dinner-hour chaos." The total cost for these meals out is $950 for the year.[9]

Professional Expenses

Betty's firm pays $120 for membership dues in a professional association for accountants. She usually does not attend the monthly dinner meetings nor the semi-annual conventions because she does not want to take any more time away from her family.

THE BOTTOM LINE

Let's look at our worksheet and see what Betty keeps of her $20,000 salary.

+	Salary	$20,000	
	Benefits	1,846*	
		– Benefit Contributions	$2,798
		– Taxes	4,457
		– Child Care	5,148
		– Household Help	0
		– Transportation	1,050
		– Clothes	500
		– Meals Out	950
		– Professional Expenses	0
THE BOTTOM LINE			$6,943

*Actual immediate cash value of benefits (for paid time off work);
the rest of the benefits value represents future protection.

Anyone who has ever filled out an IRS 1040 Form with
a fair amount of itemized deductions knows that this is just
a cursory look at some of the major points to consider in
analyzing a second income. The transportation costs and meals
out are mitigated by the fact that the family would be eating
(just less expensively) whether or not Betty worked and most
suburban families own two cars (regardless of whether the second
is used for getting a wage earner to work or transporting children
to lessons and other activities). On the other hand, the $1,846
value of the benefits is not cash in hand. The paid time off
from work has value, but you cannot spend it. Therefore, while
the bottom line of immediate cash value is $6,943, the family
will be left with $5,097 in additional disposable income.

The estimates in this illustration use conservative expense
figures. To make our calculations easier, we allowed Betty and
John to live in Texas, where there is no state income tax. The
true bottom line is that Betty is working 40 hours each week
and her family has an additional $5,097 to spend. This partially
explains why sizeable gains in gross income do not seem to
be accompanied by equivalent gains in standards of living.

On the other hand, $5,097 can make the difference between
falling behind with the bills or being on top of them. The
important point to remember is to evaluate the financial portion
of the equation based upon the difference it actually will make
to your family income, not what an interviewer quotes you across
a desk.

TAX CHANGES

These calculations were based upon 1986 tax information from
the Internal Revenue Service, the most recent instructions
available at the time this book went to print. However, the
Tax Reform Act of 1986 made sweeping changes in our tax
laws. They will not be in effect fully until 1988, but some of
the differences to look for as you calculate the financial part
of your equation are as follows:

- Tax brackets, which through 1986 ranged from 11 to 50 percent,
  have been restructured. There will be five brackets in 1987
  (11, 15, 28, 35, and 38.5 percent) and three in 1988 (15, 28,
  and 33 percent). Both ends of the spectrum have been adjusted
  toward the middle.

- The two-earner tax adjustment has been repealed.

- IRAs have been curtailed. If *either* the husband or wife is

covered by an employer-sponsored retirement plan, neither
one can take the full tax deduction on the IRA contribution
unless joint income is under $40,000. Partial deductions are
allowed if joint income falls between $40,000 and $50,000.

- Deductible contributions to 401 (k) plans have been cut back
  from $30,000 to $7,000 per year. This limit will be adjusted
  for inflation beginning in 1988.

- Most business and professional expenses will be considered
  miscellaneous expenses and are deductible only when their
  total exceeds two percent of adjusted gross income.

- The three martini lunch has been attacked. Only 80 percent
  of business meals and entertainment is deductible now.

The bottom-line effect of the tax changes is not going to
be beneficial for most dual career couples. However, another
movement in the working world just might be.

FLEXIBLE BENEFITS

For the last 15 years, flexible benefit plans, or cafeteria plans,
slowly have been gaining acceptance. With these benefit
programs, the employee is given an "allotment" and allowed
to choose needed benefits. Often, there is a certain core of
minimal benefits from which the employee cannot deviate. He
or she can change the benefit mix annually.

Today, more than 150 major firms covering over three
million workers have some type of flexible benefit plans.[10] These
plans have great appeal to dual-career couples. It allows them
to avoid unneeded duplication of certain benefits, e.g., health
insurance, and trade off for those which may be more useful,
e.g., additional time off from work. Some plans even offer child
care subsidies as an option.

Flexible benefit plans have an additional advantage to the
participants. Most plans are set up so that employee contributions to benefits are treated on a pretax basis. The employee
authorizes a "salary reduction" in the amount of his or her
contribution. This can reduce some families' tax bills
significantly.

MORE THAN NUMBERS

The numbers do not tell the whole story. There are other
considerations which do not show up so clearly in the figures.
The benefits toward which you and your employer contribute
do not end up as cash in hand, but may take care of you in
sickness, disability, unemployment, retirement, and death. The
homemaker does not have such protection in her own name.

If you can afford it and you qualify, you may make up to a $2,000 tax-deductible contribution each year to an IRA account which will provide money to you upon retirement.

In evaluating the financial portion of your equation, it is important to think of the long-term implications of your decision. Enormous child-care costs will diminish — and eventually disappear — when children enter school. Lost income needs to be evaluated in terms of the present as does how cutting back or stopping work will affect your earning ability in the future. I have known people who claim it actually costs them to work in the short term, but feel that the experience and continuous work history is necessary to get them where they want to be five or ten years in the future.

In our hypothetical example, Betty was fortunate because she had a skill that could be utilized in a small business from home. There was the option of cutting back instead of quitting altogether. This is not always the case. On the other hand, some jobs simply are not worth the investment or the sacrifices for the return. These are some issues we need to consider as we move to the professional portion of the equation.

YOUR EQUATION

The issues you should consider and may want to include in the financial portion of your equation are the following:

- Do you consider money to be the primary motivation in your work choice?

- How important is salary in a job?

- If working, are you pleased with your salary?

- Is it important for you to have your "own" money?

- Do you and your spouse generally agree on money matters?

- Is the decision-making process in your home satisfactory to you?

- Have you done a salary evaluation? If so, what was your bottom line?

- Do you worry about your personal financial security or that of your family in the future?

FOOTNOTES

[1]Chamber of Commerce of the United States, *Employee Benefits, 1985.*

[2]The figure of $5,204 is based upon the following estimated contributions:

Life Insurance at 18¢ per thousand, and coverage at two times
    salary = $72

Retirement at 7% of salary = $1,400

Paid Time Off Work of 24 days (10 vacation, 9 holidays and
    5 sick days) = $1,846

Unemployment Insurance: Federal at .08% of salary = $56.00
    and State at 1% of salary = $200

Workers' Compensation at 1% of salary = $200

FICA contribution at 7.15% of salary = $1,430

[3]The figure of $2,798 is based upon the following estimated
contributions:

Life Insurance at 17¢ per thousand, and coverage at two times
    salary = $68

Retirement at 5% of salary = $1,000

Long Term Disability Insurance = $300

FICA contribution at 7.15% of salary = $1,430

[4]This was an average of responses I got upon asking several
accountants what they thought a reasonable total of deductions would
be for a couple earning $60,000.

[5]IRS instructions for preparing Form 1040 show that tax on $46,000
is $9,629 minus tax on $28,000 which is $4,212 equals $5,417.

[6]Caroline Bird, *The Two-Paycheck Marriage* (New York: Rawson,
Wade Publishers, Inc., 1979). p. 17.

[7]The figure of $5,148 is based upon the following hypothetical
charges of $1.50 per hour per child:

40 weeks of 9 hours of day care for the younger child each
    day and 5 hours for the older child = $4,200

10 weeks of two children in family day care 9 hours per day
    each = $1350

2 weeks of vacation with no child care

minus 9 holidays at a total of $402 (2 summer and 7 school-
    year holidays)

[8]Based on IRS business allowance of 21¢ per mile.

[9]The figure of $950 is based upon the following meal cost
estimations:

1 meal out with the family per week = $10

2 meals in a cafeteria at $2 each = $4

Friday lunch with co-workers = $5

[10]Barbara Ensor Cook and Diane S. Rothberg, *Employee Benefits
for Part-Timers* (McLean, Virginia: Association of Part-Time
Professionals, 1985), p. 36.

6.
You: Professionally

It seems pretty obvious that it's good for your professional life to keep working, and detrimental when you drop out of the labor force. Therefore, it should follow that the professional component of your equation would always indicate a leaning toward working as much as possible.

The root of the working/parenting issue is the fact that these two areas so often are in conflict. Women feel as though they are forced to choose between their careers and their children. Many work environments exacerbate the dilemma by a total lack of flexibility regarding hours, leave, and doing assignments at home.

Leaving a job or cutting back on work hours does not have to mean professional suicide. Many things need to be considered. How long will the absence be? Is there a good chance of being reemployed when you want to be? Does your job require skills which "rust" quickly? Are there options for staying in touch with contacts and professional developments during your absence?

Life involves taking risks and this may be one of the biggest ones. Women who are forced into that "all or nothing" decision regarding their jobs often can not predict precisely how their decisions will affect their professional futures.

Studies have indicated that women's progress in the labor market may depend heavily upon their job attachment. In low-income families, even though there is a high labor force participation rate, women tend to work intermittently and change jobs often.[1] This results in a loss of seniority which is the main route to advancement in nonprofessional jobs.

In more affluent families, women are most likely to have a period during their childbearing years where they drop out of the work force totally or drastically reduce their work hours.

This occurs at the same point where young women on the fast track are making their biggest career leaps. When mothers have the time and energy to once again devote themselves full time to their careers, they are facing competition from a whole new generation of women. In order to combat this phenomenon, many women are postponing childbearing to first establish their careers. These women tend to return to the work force more quickly after having children, most likely because they are coming back to better jobs.

Much of the wage gap between the earnings of men and women can be explained by the career interruption experienced by women due to domestic responsibilities. Each year of unemployment results in lower earnings upon reentry. One study reported that a two- to four-year break from work lowers average earnings by 13 percent and a five-year break resulted in 19 percent lower average earnings.[2] Some women tell stories of losing jobs due to inadequate maternity leave and never being able to find another position with equivalent status, responsibility, and pay. Thus, entire careers are damaged because of a few weeks or months of absence.

Another factor which influences job attachment is frequent moves. If a woman is forced to relocate often due to her husband's job transfers, her career is likely to suffer. Studies have shown that when couples move, the husband's income usually goes up and the wife's declines.[3]

OPPORTUNITY KNOCKS

Many mothers do not plan their careers. Often circumstances occur which place them in the position of having to make a decision quickly. It may not be the ideal time from a parenting standpoint, but opportunity knocks. They find themselves at the road's fork, and it is time to make a decision and walk down one of those roads.

Diane, 37, is a medical technologist working for a hospital in York, Pennsylvania. Her children are 6 and 4 years old. She has worked various part-time schedules since becoming a mother. Because her field is a rapidly growing one, her hospital, like others, has begun to compete for outpatient laboratory work. Diane was involved in the initial marketing plan of the program. The program expanded very rapidly and she found herself with the choice of increasing her hours to full time or turning over the program she had developed to someone else.

"What I was doing expanded. From a long-term perspective and actually to establish this position for myself, I felt now was the time to go with it.

"On the other hand, I did not want to do this (work full time) until my children were both in school. So I fell short of my goal with them being 4 and 6. I needed to reconsider. It was not exactly the right time but the professional opportunity presented itself and I needed to make a decision. It was now or never."

Kathleen, 39, is a bookkeeper who went back to work when her only daughter was 8 years old (introduced on p. 61). While she had been planning a return to the labor force for many years, circumstances caused the timing.

"I had plenty of time to think about whether or not to work. What I'm doing relates to what I figured out I wanted to be doing over time. It's a direction choice.

"It's something I've been wanting to do for a long time (return to work). The fact that I have started work this year is attributable to two opportunities falling in my lap. I might still be doing volunteer work had these opportunities not presented themselves. I've wanted to do this for some time, and suddenly it was easy to do it."

FULL SPEED AHEAD

For those who do consciously plan their career commitments, what implications do the various choices have professionally? A full-time work week allows for career advancement and routine exposure to an array of work assignments, training opportunities, networking, etc. Mothers seem just like everyone else — almost.

It would be unusual if there were not some effect at work of the added responsibilities on the homefront. Rare is the woman who chooses to work through labor pains, spend one night in the hospital, and return after a few days leave, as if she had gone to the islands for a short vacation.

A recent article in a business magazine did portray a banking senior vice president who works sixty-plus hours each week and took just one week off after each of her two children was born. "If you want to make it to the top, you've got to sacrifice," she says.[4]

Thankfully, the article went on to describe a few corporate programs designed to allow women executives to slow down for awhile at least. One management consulting firm has a special long-term career plan for employees who want to work fewer hours, but eventually become partners. Consulting work, flexitime, part-time schedules, parental leave and even company-provided babysitters for business trips are being offered by innovative companies across the country.[5]

The choice to continue a career at full speed while parenting seems to work best if you have a full-time mother substitute at home. Even so, there are a few common professional problems that full-time working moms face:

Full-time Means Doing Nothing but Work

In some competitive fields, working from nine to five sounds like a vacation. Making partner in a prestigious law, accounting, or consulting firm means endless hours of work, with many nights and weekends in the office. Cutting back means stepping aside to someone who is willing to work morning, noon, and night.

The Wrong Balance

Working full time can create such stress and fatigue that you cannot perform your job to the best of your ability. Working fewer hours and doing a terrific job may help your career more than showing up every day with bags under your eyes and falling asleep during staff meetings.

Professional Commitment Questioned

Co-workers and supervisors often assume that women with families will have less dedication to their jobs than men or women without children. This assumption may lead to withheld assignments or promotions.

A hectic pace over many years can have its consequences. Laurie, 42, who has worked full time while parenting (introduced on p. 40) confessed that she had recently written away for information from a new organization called Superwomen Anonymous. When asked what effect her work decision has had upon her professional life, she replied:

> "It's been hard to be a Superwoman for 20 years. It's taken its toll. My problem is that there are so many wonderful things to do that I can't stop myself. I have written 14 children's books (in addition to my full-time job). I look back now and I can't imagine when I had time to write them.
> " . . . The whole question of being a Superwoman has to be addressed. I don't think most of us knew what we were getting into. Our responsibilities are so divided. Those of us who have chosen to have real careers also like to do other things as well. . . . It's been a constant conflict. It's hard for me to say no. There are times when I just absolutely wear myself to a frazzle. I don't know what it means to relax."

For some mothers, even working full time is not enough to keep up professionally. Deborah, 32, is an attorney with a small New York City law firm. Her first child is 20 months old and when he was born, she cut back her hours to "just" a full-time workweek. She is aware that this has been detrimental to her career and suspects that others question her professional commitment. Nevertheless, in order to keep pace with the other attorneys her age, Deborah would be left with almost no time for her child.

> "In the kind of service business I'm in, my time is not my own. It is dictated by clients' needs. I don't have the liberty of saying I'm not going to come in today and staying at home.
> "I work nine to five except in the event of an emergency. It's almost unheard of to practice corporate law in New York City and work regular hours.
> "A lot of people believe that a woman who is a lawyer with children is not serious about practicing law if she tries to keep regular (full-time) hours. . . . Most lawyers are still there at 8:00 at night and I'm long gone by then. I think, although no one has ever said it to me, in the back of their minds, they may question my seriousness.
> "I think I will probably never be a partner in this law firm or any other firm with the hours I keep. My career has suffered (by becoming a parent). But I knew that all along, that it would be one of the effects of having children. The only women I know whose careers haven't been affected are those who continue to work the long hours. Who wants that?"

HANGING IN THERE

Many women attempt to keep their careers alive and remain the primary caregivers for their children simultaneously. They may convert a job to part-time hours which they previously held. Or they may search for a new job with a flexible workweek if their former employers are unwilling to be accommodating.

Working on a reduced-hours basis generally has the effect of putting your career on hold. However, it allows you to show a continuous work history on your resumé, and you avoid many of the reentry problems we will discuss shortly. You are still in the work environment, too, so you have contact with fellow workers and developments in your field. Many have described this arrangement as the "best of both worlds."

However, women who work part time encounter many problems professionally:

Full-time Work for Part-time Pay

There is a tendency to try to keep up with those who work

full time. Part-timers often take home work, stay late on their scheduled days, and sometimes find themselves producing at a full-time level but only taking home a part-time paycheck.

Inadequate Compensation

Often, employers provide a lower hourly rate to part-time employees. Sometimes benefits are totally denied; in other cases, they are meager.

Lack of Opportunity for Advancement

Many part-timers are told (directly or indirectly) that there will be no promotions until they increase their hours. The best assignments probably will go to employees who are there all the time. It can be extremely frustrating to feel as though you are in a holding pattern as others pass you by.

Not Taken Seriously

In many fields, unless you have a change of clothes and a cot in the office, you are not considered to be professionally committed. Working part time is a declaration that there are other priorities in your life, and that may affect how your colleagues perceive you.

Job Security

Many companies have a policy of firing part-time workers first during layoffs. Even if you have worked at the same firm for many years, you may find yourself collecting unemployment before a recently hired full-timer.

On the Fringe

In addition to missed business meetings, working fewer hours usually means not fully taking part in the office social life. Some part-timers feel excluded, while others are grateful for an excuse not to attend every retirement party and birthday celebration.

Pressure to Increase Hours

Many part-timers report subtle and not-so-subtle pressure to return to a full-time schedule. Employers may view the part-time hours as an irritating accommodation they hope will be temporary. There will be a lot of pressure for the woman who constantly feels she needs to justify her work schedule or negotiate for an extension of this "privilege."

Despite the problems, many mothers report that working part time is an ideal arrangement, particularly when their children are young. Debbie, 29, of Silver Spring, Maryland, took a six-month maternity leave from the trade association where she is employed as a special projects coordinator. She kept in touch with her work from home, and when she felt her son would be comfortable with a substitute caregiver in her home, Debbie began to come into the office two days a week.

> "I went back to try it. I really felt like I would be making a mistake if I did not try to go back to such an ideal situation. I could work at home if I needed to; I could work any day of the week. I had complete flexibility — to not even try it would have been a mistake. As it's turned out, when I'm home I love it, and when I'm at work I love it.
>
> "Professionally, it's kept the doors open. If I go to apply for another job, they don't see that I've been out of the work force (for an extended time). It's also allowed me to be able to switch back from the frame of mind as a mother to the frame of mind as an employee. In seeing my friends (who stay home for awhile), they have a difficult time when they return to a professional situation."

For women who enjoy their work, there is inevitable frustration in not being able to devote as much time to their professions as they would like. Kathe, 37, is an accountant who has tried various part-time options in order to keep her career active (introduced on p. 43). She talks about some of the limitations of working part time:

> "(Working part time) has not been great for my career. It's maintained it — sort of like being in limbo. I certainly have not gotten better at what I do, and I've not been able to excel in any area. I haven't been able to become a great CPA or a great specialist in one area.
>
> "I've just been able to maintain it. Some days, I'm not even sure that I maintain it to the quality that I feel I should. The profession itself does not really lend itself to part time from a technical point of view. It's really a full-time job to keep up technically."

TIME OUT

Women who choose to devote an extended period of time to remaining at home with their children postpone their professional problems. They escape the burden of juggling two jobs, and the frequent conflicts that commitment to a career and a family bring. Nevertheless, professional issues still affect their lives:

Concerns About the Future

Very few women today expect to retire for life when they become mothers. They anticipate returning to work at some point — when the children enter preschool, elementary school, high school or college. The concern about what kind of job they can expect to have for the remaining years of their worklives is a pervasive one, affecting mothers with different degrees of intensity.

Keeping in Touch

Many mothers who have established careers prior to parenthood desire to keep in touch with developments in their fields. This is extremely challenging for homemakers who must make a concerted effort to read current literature and maintain business contacts and professional affiliations.

Some women view the decision to leave a job for full-time motherhood as a death blow for their careers. Terry, 36, of Reston, Virginia, had her only child three years ago. At the time, she was a staff manager for C & P Telephone Company, and had intended to return to her position full time. A brief return convinced her that she wanted to be at home with her child, and now she says that she hopes to remain a homemaker until her daughter finishes high school.

> "My decision certainly terminated my professional life. I suppose I could go back, but it would be at the same level or below where I was. It would take me awhile to catch up on how the industry has changed, what deregulation has done.
>
> "It puts you behind on the organizational ladder. All the people your own age have progressed beyond and you're starting all over again. (Staying at home) certainly puts a damper on your career."

Other mothers feel that their years at home with their children help clarify career goals or even add to their professional competence. Joslin, 42, of Chatham, New Jersey, was a kindergarten teacher before her two daughters, now 13 and 14 years old, were born. She wants to postpone working until her children go to college, but she is busy preparing for that fast-approaching time. Recently enrolled in a graduate program for a Masters of Social Work degree, she is exploring different options for her second career.

"In terms of teaching . . . if I went back, I would be way behind in terms of what's happened over the past few years. But I've decided that I didn't want to go back to teaching.

"I think I've used my time well at home with the kids. The reason I'm going back for a Masters in Social Work is because all of my volunteer work led me in that direction. I find when I'm in the classroom with the women who are right out of undergraduate school, I have just as much to contribute. Maybe even more because of my life experiences. The reading and the volunteer things I've been able to do have enriched my life."

REENTRY

The recent phenomenon of mothers flocking to the workplace has included many "reentry" women who have been homemakers for an extended period of time. They face a special set of circumstances as they make the transition back to full- or part-time employment. The prospect of such a drastic change often causes more alarm than the actual transition itself.

One survey of homemakers contained the question, "If offered an interesting job, would you take it?" and 58 percent of the respondents replied affirmatively. However, the unemployed women showed a greater concern about anticipated difficulties than employed women did about existing problems. The fears were very accurate though, with the potential difficulties cited including child care, dual burden, lack of flexibility in the workplace, and inability to find a desirable job.[6]

Many employers recognize that reentry women can offer advantages as workers. Managers report that they are highly motivated, stable, and dedicated employees. Older women have less distractions than mothers of young children and the uncertainties of youth are probably behind them.[7] In spite of this, reentry women face a myriad of difficulties, especially looking for that first job:

Career Goals and Interests May Have Changed

Reentry women may find themselves beginning an entirely new career in mid-life. This may mean further education, retraining, and starting at the bottom.

Age

It's a sad fact that many employers discriminate against older applicants. In addition, it may be psychologically difficult to work with younger employees who have "passed you by" professionally during your years spent out of the labor force.

Rusty Credentials

Even if you want to return to the same type of job you formerly held, you may find your skills and education need to be updated.

Lost Contacts

Career counselors tell us that 80 percent of jobs are never advertised. Reentry women need to rebuild their professional networks in order to learn about job opportunities.

Gap in Resumé

Even the best functional resumé may not hide the fact that you have not been employed for several years. While many employers give credit for volunteer experience, others may consider unpaid experience to be worthless.

Low Self-Confidence

After an extended absence from the work force, you may doubt your ability to obtain a good job and perform well. Women tend to undervalue their experiences, particularly if they are unpaid.

Unrealistic Expectations

Some reentry women have unobtainable goals regarding positions, salaries, and/or flexibility in the workplace. If you have had years of managing a household or performing responsible volunteer work, it may be hard to accept a job with less power and authority.

Job-Hunting Skills

Looking for a job is both time consuming and demanding. Job hunting itself can be a full-time job, requiring specific skills such as goal setting, research, writing, networking, and interviewing.

Adjustment

The longer you have been out of work, the more difficult it may be for you to make the transition to paid employment. You may also encounter more resistance from a family which has depended upon your services for many years.

Marie, 48, is an account representative for an advertising and marketing firm. She lives in Cedarburg, Wisconsin, and has three children, ages 20, 18, and 15. She reentered the work force several years ago, anticipating both a void in her life and increased financial responsibilities when her children would enter college. After years of volunteering, she had become increasingly restless and burned out, and felt out of touch with life.

Marie chose not to return to her former teaching career. Her skills were outdated and she did not enjoy her substituting assignments. Her first job was part time, and her experience over the past few years has been challenging:

"I still have a difficult time detaching from their (the children's) needs being more important than my work needs. I will usually put their needs before my own and when I get to work, I feel very rattled because I'm plugged into their needs so much.

" . . . (Reentry) was very frightening. I'm not the assertive type. I felt a lack of knowledge and skills that I hadn't developed for years. . . . I felt like I had a big gap to fill and didn't know if I could.

"I still feel that way often because I see a younger work force that has been better trained and is more assertive. That was never important to me . . . The passive female does not fit too well in the work world. It's been very, very difficult but very, very good for me."

ALL JOBS ARE NOT CAREERS

It is important to mention that many women work at jobs and do not pursue careers. It may be because they have other motivations for working or they do not want to devote too much time and effort to their work lives.

Edie, 44, worked very sporadically as a nurse during the years she had small children. Two years ago, with three teenagers and a son in college, she felt the desire to "get on with her own life." She took a clerical job for a securities oil and gas partnership. The job is ten minutes from her home, and she can still participate in her book club or leave work without problems if her children are sick. She's experiencing both the freedom of not being tied down by a demanding job, and the growing awareness that part of her identity is wrapped up in her work life.

"I'm really a registered nurse. The hospital close by where I probably would have gone back to work is now on 12-hour shifts and I didn't feel that I wanted to do that. I didn't want to be away that much and work that much for that amount of money. . . . This (her current job) provides me (the opportunity) to do two things at one time — run a household, do all the

things I have to, be at soccer games and still get out and do
something interesting.

"I never thought money mattered and that I was just doing
this to get out of the house. I'm beginning to learn why a salary
is important. We don't need another penny in this house, but
I would like to make more money to make myself feel good."

It is inaccurate to assume that labor force attachment is
unimportant to women holding nonprofessional jobs. In this
age of rapidly changing technology, most jobs are undergoing
continual transformations. A secretary who left her electric
typewriter ten years ago would be lost in front of a word processor
today. In addition, leaving a job means lost seniority,
inaccessibility to training and forfeited opportunities for
possible promotions.

ON THE ROAD

The woman who makes frequent moves to accommodate her
husband's career faces compounded difficulties in her choice
to work or not. A relocation absorbs a tremendous amount of
time and energy, often spanning several months of planning,
househunting, packing, moving, unpacking, adjusting, and
settling down. Support systems that have been developed both
at home and at work disappear. Few organizations offer a spouse
assistance in finding a job, so she is on her own to pick up
her career as best she can.

Phyllis, 44, is a former teacher married to a foreign service
officer. They have made several moves both in and out of the
United States during their marriage. Their only child is currently
in high school, and Phyllis recently has felt that she can now
return to the work force.

"The moves have affected me greatly. I didn't work long
enough (teaching) to have a sense of security about what I was
doing. . . . Had I continued, I would have had a better sense
of whether I liked it or not and if I knew what I was doing.
So many years have gone by; I can't go back into teaching.

" . . . Every time I began to feel that I was doing something
that I could expand upon, we're off and moving again. There
are people who just dive right in and get going again, but that's
not me. I'm slow at getting adjusted. Moving has been an
interesting experience, but very detrimental in terms of a career."

Some women experience such frustration at trying to start
over in each city that they attempt to create a career in which
they can exercise more control over their situations. Kathy, 35,
is married to a program manager with the Air Force. They have

two children, ages 10 and 6. At the first couple of posts, she was able to find part-time work as a bank teller and a teacher. Upon returning to the United States, she had difficulty finding a job and decided to work for herself marketing cosmetic products.

"I was so frustrated trying to get a job that I decided to work for myself. The amount of time I work varies according to Bob's travel. . . . I know I don't have the career I really want right now but I choose it this way because my marriage and my relationship with my husband is more important to me than a full-time career. . . . I don't think that the family unit would be as good as it is, with his schedule and all the moves. . . . This gives me the flexibility to put in as much time as I want. I'm my own boss and I can move it anytime I want.

" . . . It's a problem coming into a job and trying to fit into a system, knowing you're only going to be there a short time. Now I'm in control and I don't have to worry about it. . . . I'm working with a management that understands the problems of moving.

" . . . I set my own hours; I can take it with me and I work with whomever I want. It gives me a lot of choices. . . . I've been in this business six years and we've moved five times. It's frustrating breaking it down and starting again, but I think it's made me a better consultant."

A WORD TO THE WISE

Most women will spend more than one-half of their adult lives working. Very few individuals have the financial security to be assured they would never need to work, even in the face of a spouse's death, a lengthy illness of a family member or of an unexpected financial crisis. Professional considerations should play a part in your decision-making process, even if your immediate choice is to be unemployed.

Regardless of your choice, keep up with your profession as well as you can. Look ahead and plan where you want to be ten, twenty, or thirty years from now. Do your current activities fit into your long-range career goals? If you are dissatisfied with your field or your job, are you exploring alternatives?

Finally, homemaking *is* a career. The only difference is that you receive no compensation for your work so it can not support you or your family. It is wise to remain employable if the need ever arises. As we will see in the next chapter, our chosen profession is very much a part of defining who we are.

YOUR EQUATION

The issues you should consider and may want to include in the professional portion of your equation are the following:

- Do you want to be employed now?
- If not, how much will a break hurt your career?
- What are your chances for reentry at a later date?
- Could/Would you keep up with your field during your time at home?
- If you do want to work, is your preference for part-time or full-time hours?
- If currently working, is your employer open to the schedule you want?
- If you have to work a schedule which is not your preference, how long will it create conflict for you?
- If you are job hunting, are your goals realistic?
- If making a change seems frightening, is it possible to try it for a trial period?
- Do you feel as though you have many options and bargaining power in the work place?
- Can you be satisfied with the long-range consequences of your career choice?
- How important is your career to you?

FOOTNOTES

[1]Ralph E. Smith, editor, *The Subtle Revolution* (Washington, DC: The Urban Institute, 1979), p. 44.

[2]Sylvia Ann Hewlett, *The Lesser Life* (New York: William Morrow and Company, Inc., 1986), p. 82.

[3]Smith, *op. cit.*, p. 44.

[4]Joani Nelson-Horchler, "Babies Plus Boardrooms," *Industry Week* (January 20, 1986), 228:2, p. 29.

[5]*Ibid.*

[6]*National Survey of Working Women* (Washington, DC: National Commission on Working Women, 1979), p. 14.

[7]Carrie Tuhy, "Work Resumés at 40," *Money* (January, 1983), 12:1, p. 81.

7.
You: Personally

I'm convinced that most females are born with a little something attached to their sex-determining "Y" chromosome called the "martyrdom gene." It is embedded somewhere deep within our system, and transmits the following message: "You are not allowed to have fun until everyone near and dear to you is having fun. Not only that, *you* are the one who is responsible for their happiness!"

How terrific to be able to say instead, "I'm deeply satisfied with the major areas of my life, and feel like the various parts of my world are in good balance. My loved ones and I support each other, both in realizing our lifetime goals, and in working through the daily responsibilities."

Martyrs are not very happy people; nor are they nice to be around. It's your life; enjoy it! Don't go through day after day feeling like you are doing someone else a favor. The most common response to a martyr is guilt, not gratitude. Of course, there is a real distinction to be made between an abnormal vicarious lifestyle and positive caring and giving to loved ones or people (small children, the infirmed, etc.) who are incapable of taking care of themselves.

HAPPINESS

Happiness is not easy to define or measure. Who is happier, the mother who works or the one who stays at home? As we saw in Chapter Two, there is a paradox in how we view the roles we have chosen. On the one hand, we need to validate our choices and reaffirm why they are right. At the same time, it is easier to see why our way is harder than others' options. One survey of 110,000 working women found that 51 percent were dissatisfied with their salaries, and one-third complained that their jobs did not use their skills, they would like to quit but could not, or their jobs were boring. These figures were much higher for clerical, sales, and service workers. Still, more than half claimed that in general, they were happy with their jobs.[1]

Do homemakers score any better on career satisfaction? In the last chapter, I cited a survey of nonemployed women who were asked, "If offered an interesting job, would you take it?" Fifty-eight percent said yes.[2]

How do we measure who is happy? Can we just ask people? One measure is physical and emotional health. Homemakers are more likely to report that they are happy. However, when tested by various health measures, employed women scored better. Public Health Service data shows that employed women are ill less often than homemakers with the gap widening for older women.[3]

The National Center for Health Statistics reports that homemakers seem to be happier, but have more psychosomatic symptoms, shorter life spans, and more sick days. The one area in which they fared better than working women was that they had fewer nervous breakdowns. However, they felt more often as though one were coming on. This caused the researchers to hypothesize that working women could more easily afford to have a psychiatrist diagnose their mental illnesses.[4]

The Institute for Social Research at University of Michigan has reported that satisfaction with life is linked to education. The more education a woman has, the happier she is unless she is a housewife.[5] Education leads to higher expectations and higher expectations, if not realized, cause dissatisfaction.

Divorce could be considered an indication of unhappiness and many forces in our society are quick to blame the rising divorce rate on working mothers. The economics of a second income might provide increased freedom for unhappy couples to separate. On the other hand, an increased income could improve the standard of living and lessen financial strains on the marriage. Most studies have been inconclusive, but here are a few of the results:

- There is some evidence of higher stress in low-income families where both partners work.
- Women who perceive financial improvement in family income are less likely to divorce.
- The family is in more danger of divorce if the wife earns more than the husband.
- Small family size contributes more to the divorce than the work status of the wife.[6]

Two University of Virginia economists recently completed a 12-year study of 18,000 families. They concluded that working women were not causing divorce, but rather that the opposite was true. Increasing numbers of married women believe it is necessary to develop job skills and work for pay in light of the high number of divorces. The researchers found that certain factors, e.g., church attendance and relatives living nearby, lowered the divorce rate. However, educational achievement of either spouse and wives' employment had little effect on whether or not marriages survived.[7]

Much of the early research conducted tended to view working women and unemployed men as social problems. Many studies now are coming to the conclusion that employment is good for people regardless of sex. A study of life expectancy put housewives far down on that list, below blue-collar workers. Working women appear to be healthier and express a greater satisfaction with life and themselves.

Having a job, even a good one, does not guarantee happiness. Women's magazines currently are flooded with testimonies of high-powered female executives who confess to feeling empty, regretting the choices they have made. Neither women nor men can hope to find total self-fulfillment through careers.

One extremely valuable research project looked into the outcomes of decisions made by women now ages 35 to 55. Conducted by researchers at the Center for Research on Women at Wellesley College, it attempted to evaluate the "lifeprints" of women with three variables: employment, marital status, and children. Their conclusion was that no one lifeprint leads either to satisfaction or misery.

Two main components of satisfaction were defined:

MASTERY — What makes a woman feel good about herself as a valued member of society, and as one who is in control of her life.

PLEASURE — What makes a woman find enjoyment in her life.[8]

The group which scored highest on the mastery index was divorced working women with children. Unemployed, married women with children scored highest on the pleasure scale.

A balance between mastery (having a sense of challenge and accomplishment) and pleasure (expanding areas of intimacy) is ideal. Among the findings of the study:

• Multiplicity of roles is good for well-being.

- The best prevention against depression is fostering a sense of mastery.

- Marriage and children do not cause well-being or misery in and of themselves.

- Working hard at a challenging job is good for one's health.

- Doing and achieving are at least as important as relationships and feelings.[9]

The highest group on the combined indices of well-being are married women with children and high-prestige jobs.

So much for studies; are you truly happy with your chosen career? Statistics can tell us interesting pieces of information, but we are the best barometers of how content and satisfied we are with what we do each day.

Lynda, 39, of Santa Paula, California, juggled work and family commitments with her first two children, now ages 16 and 11. Since the birth of her third child last year, she has been a homemaker. She had been facing a growing dissatisfaction with her secretarial job, and now glows with happiness at her choice to be a full-time mother:

> "I want to raise my own children. They grow up so fast ... I look at the other two and think — where did those childhoods go? I was always hoping they would grow up quickly, and I felt torn between raising them and wanting to be in the work world . . . or have my stimulation out of the home.
> "I really missed a lot, I feel. I can hardly even remember what their childhoods were like. I'm not going to let it happen this time. I'm relishing every moment with this baby and I'm enjoying him tremendously. I have a real sense of how fast the time goes by and how fast they grow up — how wonderful and how much fun it is to have a child — how interesting they are and how boring jobs are."

Lynda does not represent a majority of working moms. One national survey indicated only 12 percent of mothers who work would rather be homemakers.[10] The survey revealed that even though working mothers now outnumber stay-at-home moms, they feel atypical. They almost universally put personal needs behind work and family responsibilities. They worry about lack of time for family and personal needs, and above all, they feel GUILTY.

GUILT

Working mothers, primarily those who work full time, seem to have cornered the market on guilt. New mothers in particular face guilt at every turn. Dr. T. Berry Brazelton, a well known pediatrician and child-development expert who has acquired some sensitivity to the plight of working mothers, points out some common features of the guilt syndrome:

- Why is she leaving her job (even temporarily)? — a man wouldn't!
- How can she leave her baby? — her mother probably didn't!
- Is the caretaker doing a good job? — or worse yet, a better job?
- If anything in the entire universe goes wrong, it's because she works!

Brazelton says that a woman who gives her child over to another caretaker, even by choice, grieves, feels helpless,and worries that the child may be endangered.[11]

There are two major types of guilt, neither of which is the exclusive property of working mothers. One type centers around the anxiety of being a good parent and being responsible for this defenseless, impressionable child. The second type is less openly discussed, but is the result of resentment about the child's demands upon your time and energy.[12] Society is quick to place the burden of youngsters' troubles and failures on parents. We too frequently accept the pointing fingers, adding our own to the condemnation.

The most common type of guilt stems from the assumption that "I alone am responsible for everything this child does and is." The feeling is so common that I suspect they must write it on your discharge papers from the hospital when you give birth. In her study of mothers, Jessie Bernard ascribes this guilt to the high standards and demands we make of ourselves and our children. Any deviation is perceived as a failure, the mother's failure. There is also guilt at reserving time for yourself because you should be "perfecting" the child.[13]

The mother certainly is viewed by the outside world as being responsible for the child's behavior. The next time you see a toddler behaving in an obnoxious manner in a public setting, see where all the glares and icy stares go — to the mom, not the child! What a responsibility! No wonder the guilt flows freely.

Women who are affected by guilt often react in one of two common ways. They can dedicate themselves constantly to the child's needs in order to say, "I'm doing all I can." Another typical way of dealing with the guilt is to rationalize their absence by stating how awful they would be if they were around the child too much. They predict martyrdom, overprotective or abusive behavior, and therefore are relieved not to be there to inflict this upon the child.

Deborah, 32, is the mother of a 20-month old son. She is an associate in a law firm in New York City (introduced on p. 75). Although she works full time, she does not put in the late night or weekend hours that many of her counterparts do. Her comments concerning guilt were very typical of what I heard from other full-time working moms:

> "I needed to assuage some guilt that I had. My husband . . . men get up in the morning and see their kids for ten minutes and come home and see them for ten minutes. So his concerns were easy to take care of. My concerns were — to what extent, if any, was my child going to suffer by my not being at home.
>
> "I think a lot of women like myself, who are working not because they have to but because they want to, have some guilt about the adverse effect on the children . . . I have to look at the positive effects of my not being there. I really believe that the time we spend — this may sound trite — is quality time. I believe that I'm a more interesting person because of the kinds of intellectual stimulation I get during the day.
>
> "I'm not really sure how I'd be 24 hours a day, seven days a week with a young child. I think everybody deals with the guilt . . . I have friends at home who feel they made the right decision, but they have many days that they're tearing their hair out at 2:00 p.m., feeling guilty for not using their skills and talents in their professions. At 2:00 p.m. I often feel guilty that I'm not at home . . . I don't think you ever feel totally comfortable with the decision."

Mothers who perceive they have no choice in their employment status deal far less with guilt. Their concerns focus more on financial needs and career advancement. They simply do not waste time justifying their employment. It was interesting to note in our conversations with women across the country, that even the most vocal opponents of working mothers felt it was acceptable "if they really had to financially."

Guilt is thrust upon parents, more specifically mothers, from all angles. Dealing with it effectively begins with distinguishing between real or imagined problems, and appropriately diagnosing the cause of each concern. We simply cannot say that troubled children are caused by working mothers. There indeed may be some effects of two-paycheck families (fatigue, stress) that may add to existing problems. However, too often working mothers are convenient scapegoats for whatever goes wrong.

A couple of studies have looked at the effects of maternal satisfaction and/or guilt upon parenting. In one project, full-time homemakers who avoided employment out of a sense of duty to their children scored the lowest on a maternal adequacy test.[15] Another study comparing homemakers who were college graduates to employed professional women concluded that the former group perceived themselves as less competent in most areas, including child care.[16]

I am reminded of a speaker I once heard discussing guilt. His comment was, "Do you know why you feel guilty? Because you are!" Guilt is not a useless emotion. A colleague of mine referred to it as the "stomach factor." When you drop that child off somewhere and get a queasy, unsettled feeling, it may be worth evaluating. We need to discern which emotions warrant attention and how to dismiss the unnecessary guilt.

One of the mothers we interviewed expressed hope that a growing acceptance of each others' choices would mean less guilt for all mothers:

> "I think it's beginning to be easier. Some of the groups advocating women's rights tend to go a little overboard. They (should) relax a little and let all women have a choice. They (homemakers) shouldn't have to feel guilty about staying home. If that's what the woman wants to do, I think we're fortunate to have a choice! If she wants to stay at home and be a full-time wife and mother — fine, it's wonderful. If she wants to work full time, she shouldn't feel guilty about that, especially if her mother never did that. We shouldn't be made to feel guilty about what we choose to do, especially if we can balance it and work it into our family lifestyles and if everyone is happy with it in the immediate family."

STRESS

In some old notes I found someone's list of the major sources of stress in our lives which include:

- Major role conflicts between career, family, and personal needs.
- Too many changes at one time, e.g., new baby, new job, move.
- Demands of other people on us and our own expectations.

It is easy to see why many women walk around with high stress levels.

No one gets through life without encountering difficult, stressful situations, but constant stress is a serious condition. It may lead to an increase in disease risk factors and mental health problems. Early stress research focused on men and identified the workplace as the source of primary stressors. Home was viewed as a sanctuary. This assumption was also continued as women entered the work force.[16]

Occupational stress for men and women is similar; work overloads, responsibilities, and deadlines are common to many professions. However, women tend to hold the majority of low-paying, low-skill jobs, and may have the added stress factor of lack of control over their work pace and environment. These jobs combine a high level of demand with a low degree of autonomy.

Insurance actuaries predicted that as women made inroads into high-status occupations, their health problems and mortality rates would begin to resemble men's. Instead studies have indicated that employment has positive effects on women's mental and physical health.[17] Work may actually serve as a buffer against the stress from other roles. The Lifeprints Study concluded that motherhood was the greater cause of stress, control, and structure. On the other hand, the sheer time commitment of doing two full-time jobs at home and at the office takes its toll.

Homemakers share some of the worst features of dissatisfying employment: repetitiveness, monotony, and the endless amount of housework. No one can deny the noise level, fatigue and daily stress experienced as a result of being with young children all day. The stress is magnified by the total lack of support for mothers at home. Jessie Bernard claims that our society has institutionalized and glorified motherhood, but left mothers as the sole caretakers in an isolated household with no help. This exclusive responsibility for caregiving is unique in history, and not particularly good for the mother or the child. Research has indicated that in cultures where mothers bear the greatest responsibility for child care they are more changeable in expressing warmth, more likely to have hostilities unrelated to the children's behavior, and unstable in their emotional reactions to children.[19]

Homemakers exhibit more anxiety about child raising. They are more reluctant to share the decision-making process with others and are more protective of their children than working women.[20] It is not clear whether this is caused by increased exposure to the child or whether women who exhibit these characteristics choose to be homemakers.

While there is some dispute about which mothers are under the most stress, almost everyone agrees that the most difficult years are when the children are young. In the Lifeprints Study, the very group you would think would be under the most stress (married women with children holding high-prestige jobs) scored the highest on well-being. A Boston University study looked into life stress, depression, and illness, and found that married career women with children were the least depressed or ill in response to stress.[21]

There are several hypotheses for why working women seem to score better on these studies:

- The rewards of employment outweigh problems.
- Working (leaving home) makes it easier to cope with family stress.
- Work is a buffer and an escape from all kinds of tension.
- Working women do not feel as obligated to do as much for their families.
- Employment is a convenient excuse to drop unwanted outside obligations.[22]

Lisa, 31, is the mother of a 4-year-old daughter. She is a homemaker in Marietta, Georgia, and plans to return to her career as a pediatric nurse practitioner in the future. She spoke about the types of stress that mothers must choose between:

> "When women stay at home they end up taking on more needs of the child and husband . . . Men should also be concerned about (family needs) but women at home tend to carry the majority of that burden themselves. By the same token, women who work tend to shoulder these burdens alone also.
>
> "That went into my decision-making. I knew that if I continued to work that I would probably have the responsibility of my child, my home, and my career . . . Something or somebody suffers (from the overload) and it's usually the woman . . . That's the hardest part abut going back to work; you're just stretched very thin. You're trying to keep everybody happy — your husband, your child, and the people at your job. You neglect yourself.
>
> "In some ways women at home have it more difficult. You don't have the option of getting away from the child . . . It's a 24-hour thing that never ends. The responsibility for the child and the home is always there. When you work, you turn over part of the responsibility and stress to a substitute caregiver."

In addition to the stress of doing, there's the stress of change and choice. Drastic change usually occurs when a woman stays home after many years of working or vice versa. The stress comes mostly from fears in three areas:

- Fear of disruption of family routine.
- Fear of submergence in family or work.
- Fear of uncertainty about future.[23]

Much of the anxiety centers around how family roles will change. There is also stress concerning whether or not the change is leading the woman down a route she may regret and how she will adjust to her changed image.

Choices for my generation have been difficult. I confess to fearing that the choices for our daughters may be even more stressful. More education is required to compete for good jobs. A Master's degree today is equivalent to the Bachelor's degree of our parents' generation. Women are postponing marriage and childbearing in order to first establish their careers. The biological timeclock remains fixed and fertility problems are increasing at an alarming rate. In brief, there is a shortened time span to make critical choices, many of which can not be reversed. Then we spend the rest of our lives living with them.

Two mental health studies conducted in the 1950s and repeated in the 1970s produced interesting results. The Midtown Manhattan Longitudinal Study and a project sponsored by the National Center for Health Statistics revealed that women's overall mental health has improved. However, stress is greater, particularly in younger women. They feel a tremendous pressure and expectation to "do it all."

There are several options for coping with stress:

- Change or ignore the expectations of others.
- Change your own attitude and expectations.
- Accept the various demands and find ways to meet them.

Translating this to a work-choice context, the positive options are to make a decision which limits stress factors for you or to accept a demanding situation but learn to control it.

SELF-IMAGE

A healthy self-image is extremely important to our well-being. Do you like who you are? Part of who you are is what you do. Your chosen occupation helps define your image both to yourself and to others. A negative self-image can be extremely detrimental to your self-satisfaction, even if you are engaged in work you enjoy. If you are convinced the work is not valued, there is an ongoing conflict.

Certain people have incredibly healthy self-images and do exactly what they want to do with little concern for how society or other people view them. Unfortunately, most of us are not so secure and we rely, to some degree, on the opinions of others to help us determine how we rate in various areas.

What other forces are there which shape our self-image? "Society" is a rather vague term which probably can be pragmatically defined by what the media presents and how the "person on the street" responds. While there is undoubtedly a war still in progress over women's roles, most women now feel that society has bestowed its blessings upon the career woman.

Dottie, 28, is a homemaker and the mother of two preschoolers with a third child on the way. She moved to Reston, Virginia, a suburb of Washington, DC, nearly three years ago. Her old neighborhood was filled with young mothers at home with their children. "Big city life" has been a difficult transition for Dottie. While she is happy and comfortable with her choice to be at home with her children, she admits to feeling out of step with "today's woman."

> "Society does not support my goals at all. (It perpetuates) the image of the housewife at home eating bon-bons and watching the soaps. But the woman of the 80's does it all — she works, takes wonderful care of her children, and is great in bed to boot. The picture of the way a woman should be is definitely not me and also is not very realistic. The perfect 80's American woman certainly needs to work."

Another evaluation to be considered comes from the "experts." They may be sociologists, pediatricians, child-development specialists, educators, career planners, or psychologists. If you look long enough, you can find almost any kind of expert to validate your choice. On the other hand, if you take any of it too seriously, you are bound to be plagued by uncertainty. For example, in an article on the erosion of the American family, child-development expert Urie Bronfenbrenner cites the dual-career family and the empty home as a reliable predictor of trouble, including reading difficulties, truancy, dropping out of school, drug addiction, and childhood depression. To be fair, he does not lay this all at the feet of women. The guilt is shared by the entire family, changing neighborhoods, inflexible workplaces, and an indifferent society. Nevertheless, few working women would come away from the article feeling like they were making a positive contribution to their families or society.

On a more personal level, the opinions of your friends and loved ones are even more influential in affecting your self-image. In subsequent chapters we will examine the effects of their input upon your decision. Briefly, the closer the individual is to you, the more critical the problem is if your basic beliefs, goals, and attitudes are not compatible.

Your self-image is important not only for how it makes you feel about yourself, but for what you want to project to others. The group that women seem most concerned about is their children. They want their choice to result in positive role modeling.

Arlene, 32, lives in Phelps, New York and commutes two hours a day to her job as a buyer in a department store. She has maintained a full-time career through the births of her daughter age 3 and son, 6 months. Arlene feels that her daughter may not have a choice about working and wants to present a positive image of a working mother.

> "I'm satisfied and we have good dinner conversation. My husband and I are still interested in each other and I'm not obsessed with the children and the house and schedules and food and drapes and groceries and things like that. I think it (working) makes me more interesting and makes life better for my husband and my family.
>
> "As my daughter becomes older, two-income families will become almost mandatory. It's a good role model for her. She talks about going to meetings now, and she wants to go see my office and get her own desk in the house. I think I'm a good role model if this is something she opts to do, or may very well have to do in the future."

Images can change. The psychological theory of cognitive dissonance states basically that we can not tolerate the conflict of living or acting in a way that is contrary to our beliefs. If that condition persists too long and we cannot change our actions, then we will change our beliefs to bring them into conformance with our behavior. This was borne out in our discussions with women who found themselves in a role previously unimagined. Like reformed smokers or alcoholics, they became the most vehement defenders of their choices, be it homemaker or employed woman.

YOUR EQUATION

The issues you should consider and may want to include in the personal portion of your equation are the following:

- Are you happy with what you are doing?
- Is this choice best for you or best for other people?
- From which areas of your life do you derive pleasure?
- From which areas of your life do you derive a sense of accomplishment?
- Do you feel guilty about anything?

- If so, is it the result of a real problem and can it be dealt with?

- Do you feel under a constant state of stress?

- If so, has it reached a level which affects your physical or mental health?

- Does the stress come from a single source or mere overload?

- Are you agonizing over a change or a choice to be made?

- Do you have a positive self-image?

- What or who affects your image of yourself?

- Are you proud of what you do?

- Would you like your daughter to repeat your choice in the future?

FOOTNOTES

[1]National Commission on Working Women, "National Survey of Working Women," (June, 1979), p. 2.

[2]*Ibid.*, p. 14.

[3]Caroline Bird, *The Two-Paycheck Marriage* (New York: Rawson, Wade Publishers, Inc., 1979), p. 35.

[4]*Ibid.*

[5]*Ibid.*, p. 41.

[6]Ralph E. Smith, ed., *The Subtle Revolution* (Washington, DC: The Urban Institute, 1979), p. 109.

[7]Patricia Nicholas, "Working Women and Divorce: Cause or Effect?" *Psychology Today* (October, 1986), 20:10, p. 12.

[8]Bureau of Labor Statistics, Department of Labor, "Employment in Perspective: Women in the Labor Force," Report 725, 1985, p. 61.

[9]Grace Baruch, Rosalind Barnett and Caryl Rivers, *Lifeprints* (New York: New American Library, 1985), p. 1.

[10]*Ibid.*, p. 14.

[11]Jane Anderson, "Making Multiple Roles Easier for Working Mothers," *Christian Science Monitor* (June 20, 1983), p. 16.

[12]Terri Minsky, "Advice and Comfort for the Working Mother," *Esquire* (June, 1984), 101:6, p. 157.

[13]Francine S. Hall and Douglas T. Hall, *The Two-Career Couple* (Reading, Massachusetts: Addison-Wesley Publishing Co., 1979), p. 133.

[14]Marlyn Harris, "The Three Career Life," *Money* (May, 1985), 14:5, p. 79.

[15]Gloria Norris and Joann Miller, "Motherhood and Guilt," *Working Woman* (April, 1984), p. 159.

[16]*Ibid.*

[17]Grace Baruch, "Integrating the Study of Women and Gender in to Research on Stress," *Research Report* (Fall, 1985), 5:1, p. 3.

[18]*Ibid.*

[19]Harris, *op. cit.,* p. 109.

[20]Ellen Goodman, *Turning Points* (Garden City: Doubleday & Co., Inc., 1979), p. 233.

[21]Baruch, *Lifeprints, op. cit.,* p. 144.

[22]*Ibid.*

[23]Goodman, *op. cit.,* p. 163.

8.
Your Child

I defy anyone to find a mother who would willfully choose a course of action that was detrimental to her child. We all want what is best for our children, including the highest quality child care. So what is best, a mom who is unemployed or one who works part time or full time?

STUDIES AND EXPERTS

Good luck if you hope to find an answer from the experts, or in the countless research studies which have been conducted on the effects of maternal employment on children. The experts disagree and the studies yield few conclusive results. Nevertheless, I will give a brief summary of what the major voices in this debate are saying.

A hero of homemakers is Dr. Burton White, a well-known pediatrician, who has concluded that full-time substitute care for children under 3 is not in their best interests.[1] He suggests that the early years are extremely critical and that somewhere between the first and third birthdays, one can predict where the child is headed in later life.[2] According to Dr. White, the best option for a child is to spend most of his or her waking hours with a member of the nuclear family. He worries about the effects on children when both parents work, the pressure at home, and the mothers and fathers who are missing the joys of parenting. He feels that part-time alternative care, however, may be conducive to a better parenting experience.[3]

Dr. Urie Bronfenbrenner's formula for children is good quality care and a substantial amount of time with someone "who is crazy about him."[4] This type of irrational commitment can not be purchased, he says. Dr. Bronfenbrenner also warns about the dangers of too much time with Mom, and suggests that the child needs a little of everything: Mom, Dad, relatives, peers, and strangers.[5]

The latest voice in the conflict is Eleanor Weisberger, an assistant professor of child therapy at Case Western Reserve University School of Medicine. Her most recent book, *When Your Child Needs You,* also sets apart the first three years of the child's life as the time to become attached to one or two caretakers. Weisberger claims that society has changed, but children have not. Preschoolers need "quantity time, so that the mother is on hand to fulfill a need at the moment it is necessary."[6]

Working mothers can find comfort in the studies of Dr. Jerome Kagan, Harvard child-development researcher. At a university-run day-care center in Boston, he found that infants and toddlers developed emotionally and cognitively in the same way as a carefully matched group of "home-bred" children.[7] Dr. Kagan further concluded that children tended to be more like their parents, even when they spent the majority of their time with substitute caregivers. The day-care children acted and spoke like their parents and formed the same strong bonds of attachment as children with full-time mothers. In times of stress, or when the children were tired or bored, they turned to their biological mothers, not the caregivers.[8]

A research team at the University of Arizona surveyed 6,000 pediatricians to get their opinions on children of working mothers. Most reported few differences between children in terms of child development, academic difficulties, or emotional problems. Two-thirds did report that children in day care develop more acute infections. When asked how old the child should be when the mother returns to work, the responses were:

3 months or less	7%
3 years	26%
When child begins school	36%
It doesn't matter	29%
Never	1%[9]

Some researchers even change their minds. Ten years ago, psychologist Jay Belsky of Penn State University co-authored a report which concluded that young children fared equally well at home or in a substitute care situation. In 1986, he published an article claiming that new evidence showed that children in substitute care are more likely to be aggressive and uncooperative in school. He warned that babies who spend more than 20 hours per week away from their mothers during the first year of life may have insecure attachments to them.[10]

Most of the research studies attempting to measure the effects of maternal employment of children have been conducted within the last ten years. As the "working mother trend" became apparent, many alarmists pointed to Harlow's monkeys and Bowlby's orphans to warn that a generation of children would be damaged. Psychologist Harry Harlow separated infant rhesus monkeys and reared them in isolation. The monkeys huddled in the corners of their cages and languished. As adults, they were unable to interact with other monkeys, were not sexually receptive, and failed to mother occasional offspring.[11]

John Bowlby was an English psychologist who conducted a study of orphans raised in British institutions following World War II. While the infants received minimal care and had clean surroundings, they were rarely held by the nurses. These babies stopped eating and playing, rarely even glancing up from their cribs.[12] Many feared that children in day care would be unable to develop bonds with parents or peers and that their growth would be delayed physically and mentally.

Substitute care can not be equated with being locked in a cage alone or being left in a crib all day. In the intervening decade, researchers have attempted to measure physical, intellectual, and social development of children. Unfortunately, the variables of child rearing are so interlocked that it is not reliable to point to the outcome and know for certain the cause.

In 1980, a Panel on Work, Family, and Community was established by the Committee on Child Development Research and Public Policy with the support of the National Institute of Education, U.S. Department of Education. Its charge was to conduct a scholarly review of what was known about the outcomes of changes in parental employment and its effect upon children. The Panel's answer was that work is not a single uniform condition and it may lead to different consequences in different circumstances.[13] They refused to make a judgment on whether or not working parents are good or bad for children. Their answer was that it depends, on the parent, the child, the circumstances, and so forth.[14]

A follow-up review by the same panel concentrated on school-age children and their findings were similar. Income, race, family structure, special characteristics of the child, and supportive services available to the family seem to be more significant than the mother's employment status.[15] How, where, and with whom these children spent their time depended on social, economic, cultural, and ideological factors, not working parents. If the parents both worked, there was less time spent together, but no less time in mutually shared activities.[16]

Some studies have concentrated on more narrowly focused outcomes for children. No one has proved any major differences in physical development. Several research projects document that young children in day care are more susceptible to contagious diseases.[17] Coughs, colds, sore throats, and chicken pox that felled my generation in kindergarten and first grade now wipe out day-care centers and preschools. Other reports cite day-care centers as "major hotbeds" for the spread of more serious diseases, such as hepatitis A, meningitis, and diarrheal diseases.[18] The National Center for Health Services Research conducted a study of 5,000 children ages 1 to 11 and claimed that children of working mothers were no more likely to get sick and stay home from school than children of homemakers.[19]

Most research on intellectual development shows little difference; preschoolers have equivalent scores in terms of memory, concept formation, vocabulary, and language comprehension. However, one national study funded by the Department of Education concluded that children from single-parent homes and from homes where mothers worked scored lower on achievement tests than counterparts from "traditional" homes. A distinction was made between income levels. For higher-income families, the additional income did not seem to be offset by the loss of time. There was the opposite effect on low-income families. The additional money made more of a contribution to the child's achievement.[20]

Mothers in the work force received good news from a major study released last year which concluded that their children scored higher in math and reading, had a lower absentee rate, and were more self-reliant than children of nonworking mothers. John Guidubaldi, a Kent State psychologist who co-authored the five-year study, said that these youngsters scored higher on IQ tests, had better communication skills, were more involved in school activities, and were rated higher in achievement by their teachers. Distinctions also were made between children of working mothers. The children fared best when the mother worked part time, was married, had a high status job with flexible hours, and was satisfied combining dual roles.[21]

The New York Infant Day Care Study, a longitudinal comparative field study of 31 day-care programs confirmed some positive effects of day care for low-income children. Over 400 children were studied from birth to age 3. On all measures, the day-care children scored as well or better than home-reared counterparts.[22]

Differences in socialization skills are most marked and the tests are also the most subjective. Children in day care are more independent and less likely to stay close to a parent in an unfamiliar setting. They become more socialized to peers and have less interaction with adults. Their behavior is more outgoing, sometimes channeled in a cooperative way, but also in a boisterous or aggressive manner at times. One study indicated fifteen times the amount of aggressive behavior (measured by verbal abuse and direct hitting or pushing) in day-care children.[23]

How these socialization skills are interpreted depends much upon the bias of the individual observing them. One researcher concluded that the independent, aggressive and outgoing behavior would enable these children to be better adjusted when beginning school and more likely to be leaders.[24] Another predicted that the activity level combined with a low frustration tolerance and lack of self-control would contribute toward a poor start in school.[25]

A final note of interest concerning research studies is that there has been some consensus that boys are more negatively affected by a mother's absence than girls. Daughters of working mothers are more independent and career oriented, and have less traditional views of marriage and sex roles.[26] Boys tend to demonstrate the differences in social skills more dramatically with increased aggressive behavior, nonconformance to parental requirements and a greater likelihood of submitting to peer influence.[27] One study indicated lower academic performance in grade school and increased vulnerability to the ill effects of family stress.[28] However, a positive outcome for boys was that they took on more household responsibilities.[29]

These studies all have obvious limitations. First of all, they look at day-care center children, and only a small percentage (approximately 15 percent) of substitute child care is provided in centers. The centers are usually well funded, often set up solely for the study. The measures of outcome are far from scientific. Finally, it is impossible to isolate the day-care factor as a cause of behavior.

After eight years of reading innumerable studies like those mentioned above, as a layperson, I have come to the following conclusions:

- Happy mothers are good mothers.
- Stress is bad for the entire family. It is not the exclusive property of working mothers or homemakers.
- Children who start day care at a young age are more likely to catch contagious ailments earlier and more frequently.

- The parent-child bond is strong and unique; it will not be diminished by day care.

- Full-time day care helps children who come from home environments which are not nurturing.

- Intellectual ability is not significantly affected by day care.

- Socialization skills are speeded up in day-care children. This has positive and negative effects.

- Children in day care have less interaction with adults and increased peer exposure. This has positive and negative effects.

CHILD CARE

Over and over, I heard the phrase, "I could never work if it weren't for my housekeeper/my sitter/my day-care center." No mother will ever feel comfortable about working unless she is convinced that her child is receiving good substitute care. There are three major alternatives:

- *In-Home Care.* The substitute caregiver comes to your home. It may be a relative, nanny, housekeeper, or babysitter.

- *Family Day Care.* The substitute caregiver watches one or more children in her own home.

- *Center.* A center usually handles larger numbers of children. It may be nonprofit or for profit, and may be located in a church, office, shopping center, converted home, etc.

There are pros and cons for each childcare situation. Some of the advantages and disadvantages are outlined below:

In-Home Care

Pros

- Cheaper for three or more children.

- Attention of caregiver focused solely on your children.

- Infants, toddlers, and special-needs children may benefit from this type of care.

- Care might be provided at unusual hours.

- Caretaker may help with household chores.

- Sick children can remain at home.

- Children do not have to be taken out early, on bad weather days, etc.

Cons

- Expensive; in addition to minimum wage, you must pay Social Security and unemployment taxes.
- Trust and faith is placed on one individual who is not supervised.
- Children are not exposed to peers regularly.
- May offer less stimulation.
- Crisis when sitter gets sick or quits.

Family Day Care

Pros

- Child is still in home environment.
- Other children are available for interaction.
- Flexible hours.
- Cost effective for one or two children.
- May eliminate transportation problems for school-age children.

Cons

- Trust and faith is placed in one individual who is not supervised.
- Vast majority of family day care is not licensed or inspected.
- Provider will give priority to own children.
- Crisis when sitter gets sick or quits.
- Caretaker may not want sick children.
- Other children may not be same age or may not be a good influence.

Center

Pros

- Always open during normal business hours.
- Can guarantee same environment over a long period of time.
- May meet certain religious or educational preferences.
- Supervised, licensed, and inspected.
- Should have standards for teachers.
- Other children of the same age present.

Cons

- Larger number of children.
- Will not accept sick children.
- Usually take only toilet-trained children.
- Not a home atmosphere.
- May have more than one shift of caretakers.
- May provide an overload of group interaction.
- Set schedules may not appeal to certain types of children.

Within each category, there are also various alternatives. Many of the successful group efforts are parent cooperatives. In some cases, parents actually take turns providing the care. In others, they run the group as a business, and directly manage staffing, purchasing, scheduling, etc.

A fast-growing alternative in my area is the use of au pairs. Au pairs generally are European girls between the ages of 18 and 25 who live with an American family for one year. They receive a small salary, plus room and board. Most au pair arrangements focus almost exclusively on child care, not housework. Many arrangements are set up informally through networking or placing advertisements in foreign newspapers. There are also organizations in this country (The Experiment in International Living, American Institute for Foreign Study, etc.) which run government-approved programs. Under the new immigration law, it is critical to verify that the girls have proper documentation before bringing them into the country.

There are good and bad examples in each category. Which alternative is best for your child depends on many factors: age, personality, length of time that substitute care is required, logistics, etc. Your priorities may change with time.

Deborah, 32, is a full-time attorney in New York City (introduced on p. 75). Her criteria for child care for her two-year-old son are quite different than those she had when he was an infant.

"Our concerns are different now. When you have a three-and-a-half-month-old child, you want someone to take care of his physical needs in a loving and caring way. Is the caretaker going to be intelligent and responsible enough so I don't sit at my desk in Manhattan, 50 minutes away, worrying what would happen in an emergency?

"Now my husband and I are reanalyzing our situation. Our concerns are very different. I have a housekeeper now and I have no doubt that she could handle an emergency or meet his physical needs. Now I think, is she reading to him? Is she teaching him? Is she showing him pictures and explaining different colors to him?"

There are certainly some common components of quality child care regardless of age or circumstances. Sandra Scarr is a University of Virginia professor who has pursued her career while raising four children. In her book, *Mother Care, Other Care,* she relates both good and bad personal experiences with substitute caregivers. Nevertheless, she believes that children can thrive with good day care or an attentive mother. She lists some requirements for a nurturing environment and believes if these elements are present, the child will do well:

- Experienced and trained caregiver.
- Small adult/child ratio.
- Appropriate experiences.
- Attention to needs of individual child.
- Physical care.
- Quiet moments.
- Boundaries and limitations.
- A speaking social partner.[30]

SNOWFLAKES

Just as each child-care situation needs to be evaluated, each youngster has a unique set of needs. No two children are alike and it is unwise to assume what works well for one can be applied to the next. Your neighbor's child may love a certain school or home that your child may hate. If you have more than one child, they may have very different personalities and needs.

My son was somewhat tentative in new surroundings and was introduced to other caretakers very slowly. My daughter adapts to change readily and is extremely sociable. I am convinced she could switch sitters each week and love it.

When I chose a nursery school for my son, it had a very open environment and a schedule that allowed plenty of free playtime. The teacher managed to keep order with her charges (mostly wild little boys) and they had a great time. My daughter's needs were entirely different. I felt she would benefit by more structure and not so much noise. She was also ready for some academic instruction that would have been totally inappropriate for my son at the same age.

Your own conclusions about what is best for children, specifically your child, may be influenced by many different sources. Lisa, 31, is a former pediatric nurse practitioner (introduced on p. 93) who felt strongly that she would be the primary caregiver in her child's preschool years.

> "The choice for me to stay home in part was due to my career. . . . I did a lot of studying about children and knew a lot about children prior to having a child. I felt that it was very important for a child to have a parent, be it mother or father, at home with him.
>
> ". . . The early years of a child's life are the most important. I think that their personalities are basically formed by the time they are three or four years old. I think it's tremendously important to have the stability of one caretaker with them for the majority of that time."

Many women with young children seemed to view the big choice as a temporary one, until Johnny or Susie reach first grade. Then, of course, they definitely would work. Mothers of older children often indicated that while the needs of school-age children were certainly different, it was still an agonizing decision. Joslin, 42, is a homemaker in Chatham, New Jersey who has recently started graduate school (introduced on p. 78). She speaks of her continuing commitment to be available for her two teenage daughters:

> "I came this far with the kids. At one point, I thought when they got to be teenagers, it would be easy to make a decision about going back to work. With teenagers, it seems that I'm needed just as much in other ways; not in answering physical needs, but in being there when school is out because they come bursting in the door with tremendous problems or great ecstasy. It would be different if I saw them at the end of the day.
>
> ". . . I still want to be available. I'm concerned about all the things that go on in homes where there are teenagers and parents are absent. When they were little, it was answering physical needs. Now it's answering emotional needs and just being on top of things. I'm not willing at this point in time to abandon all that I have done; I'm going to see this thing through."

ROLE MODEL

In the last chapter, we discussed the fact that part of a positive self-image entailed being pleased with the type of example you set for your child. To carry that thought one step further, many women decide that part of their choice should be determined by the role that they consciously set forth for their children to model.

Kathy, 35, markets women's cosmetics (introduced on p. 82) and feels that it is important to demonstrate to her children that women can parent and work, with advantages to the entire family:

> "The children see Mother in a different light. She can go out there and have a career and do something different than just staying at home. She can increase their standard of living and allow them to do the extra things they couldn't as a one-income family. She can alleviate the stress that a father would feel as a sole breadwinner.
>
> ". . . In my daughter's kindergarten class, the children were asked what they wanted to be when they grew up. There were two little girls out of 15 who wanted to be mothers. The others said, tennis teacher, nurse, doctor, etc. They had all of these ideas about what they wanted to do besides being a wife and mother. I think that's good."

SUPPORT FROM CHILDREN

Children have minds of their own. When they are young enough, they may not be able to voice their thoughts, but they have ways of letting you know whether or not they are happy. Most young children go through certain stages of separation anxiety and will cry when their parents leave them. This certainly does not indicate a dreadful day-care situation. Many a substitute caretaker has assured concerned parents that as soon as they are out of sight, the child stops crying.

It is difficult to measure how supportive very young children are. They manifest their own contentment and do not spend a lot of time philosophizing about long-term effects of maternal employment. Preschoolers, who do not have strong peer relationships yet, probably want as much time and attention as they can get from their parents, regardless of work status.

Many women claim that their children accept their work choices simply because it has always been that way. They have nothing to compare it to, and probably think all children's lives are the same. One homemaker reported her four-year-old rushed in from nursery school one day in disbelief over the fact that some of his classmates did not have mommies at home and that they went to someone else's house everyday after school!

By the time children reach school, they are aware that some mothers are employed and some are not. Their understanding of the motivations behind their mothers' decisions is increasing, but they still are likely to react to "Mom's work" based upon how it affects them.

Suzie, 37, returned to work part time for financial reasons after she and her husband separated (introduced on p. 52) Her two boys often complain about getting up early or going to a sitter's house. However, the older boy, a first grader, also thinks beyond the momentary inconvenience:

> "They understand the reasons that I'm working and I think they'd like to be supportive, but they're children. They primarily see the disadvantages.
> "When Josh thinks of his karate outfit or our VCR, he looks at that and says, 'If that's the reason you're going today, then it's okay.' If it has something to do with him. The idea of buying a tire for the car, that wouldn't do it."

As children approach the teenage years, there may be dramatic changes in their attitudes toward working parents. Children are expected to accept more responsibilities around the home as they grow older. Many families hold regular meetings to divide household chores. Increasing numbers of teenagers work, some for spending money and others to contribute to the family income. Young people who are earning paychecks or helping with home responsibilities are more likely to support and respect parents engaged in similar activities.

Teenagers are extremely peer oriented and most of them are also in the process of defining who they are apart from their families. Some relish a growing sense of independence. They become quite conscious of what determines someone's place in society. One mother, a homemaker, reported that her daughters and their friends compared what their mothers did the way they compared clothes, houses, and boyfriends. She added that in their minds, being a homemaker was synonymous with doing nothing.

Joleen, 38, has worked full time since her children were preschoolers (introduced on p. 59). A couple of years ago, she took a step backwards in her career for a job closer to her home which would allow her more time with her family. She

says that her children, now teenagers, show increasing support
for her choice to work.

> "We've discussed my work with the kids. I've noticed a big
> difference the last couple of years. Jeff, the younger, always wanted
> me home. The last couple of years, they changed their attitudes,
> which in turn has affected mine. I enjoy working and having
> my own corner of the world. . . . They have adjusted their lives
> around my working. I think they enjoy some of the time on
> their own. . . . Now that they're happy, it's eased some of the
> guilt for me.
> ". . . My daughter is a more literal, pragmatic person. It's
> been real easy for her to see what we can do when I work and
> what the tradeoffs are. She's very independent; fine on her own.
> Jeff is much more dependent and needs the emotional support
> of someone there. . . . You don't have to be right beside him,
> but he wants to know you're there. It's changing as he matures
> and he's much more supportive now."

DEMANDS FROM CHILDREN

Infants and toddlers primarily need a loving person to attend
to their needs. From age 3 on, there should be a good balance
between time spent with other children and time with adults.
Just what that balance is depends upon the individual child.
Some children are extremely sociable and thrive with a large
amount of interaction with peers as well as a variety of
"extracurricular" activities. Others need heavy doses of quiet
time and prefer interacting primarily in small group situations.

All parents face daily demands from children, regardless
of whether or not the mother works. Until adolescence, it is
normal for children to want their parents around as much as
possible; not necessarily for direct interaction, but to attend to
their needs. The most vocal resistance to women's work choices
comes from children who are adjusting to change. In most cases,
this is a child whose mother has reentered the work force or
significantly increased her hours on the job.

Kathleen, 39, returned to work this past year (introduced
on p. 61). Her daughter is in third grade and Kathleen works
only while she is in school. Her work commitment does not
affect the actual time Kathleen has with her daughter and she
feels that the added dimension to her life is good for her daughter
to witness.

"I feel Kate is better off with a mother who works part time. She is an only child and she gets an enormous amount of attention from my husband and me. She is privileged and I think that she is shocked that I spend my days doing something other than sitting at home thinking about her.

"The only way that my working has affected her thus far is that I am later getting into the carpool line. So she is not one of the first people picked up on my days to drive. That's the only thing that she's thrown back at me as being a terrible strain for her."

"I think it's very good for her to have a mother who has other thoughts and concerns. I always have had them, but she hasn't thought about it in the same kind of way. I think it's important (for her) to grow up knowing that I can earn money and that I have areas of my life that I'm working on."

Older children go beyond merely expressing discontent at the inconveniences a working mother may cause them. Their behavior may be manipulative, exploiting possible indecision or guilt feelings the mother may be experiencing. Edie, 44, is the mother of four children (introduced on p. 81). She returned to work two years ago when the youngest children, twins, were in junior high school.

"I could see that the children did not need my presence as much and it was important for me to get on with some of the things I wanted to do with my own life. At 12 or 13, they didn't need me there every minute. In fact, sometimes I felt like a detriment. I needed to start looking ahead and see what I wanted to do with myself when they didn't need me anymore.

"I find sometimes that the kids use it (her working) to try to make me feel guilty and it doesn't work because I was home with them for so long. They can't pull that on me. The youngest ones say, 'Well, you're never here,' and they're really only without me an hour. . . . They seem to know what's going to make me feel guilty and they try to use it, as good teenagers do. But I tell them it's not working, and they're going to have to try something else."

Demands from children may be an expression of bona fide needs or a manipulative attempt to be the center of attention. Only the parent knows for sure!

YOUR EQUATION

The issues you should consider and may want to include in your equation are the following:

- What do you think the effects of alternative child care would be/are upon your child?

- Which type of alternative child care would you prefer, if any? Is it available to you?

- Do you anticipate that your child will require a different type of care in the future?

- What is the best amount of alternative care for your child?

- If you have more than one child, is the same type of care best for both/all?

- Do you consciously seek to present a role for your child? If so, are you succeeding?

- Do you receive support from your child for your current choice?

- Is there active resistance to your current choice?

- How would your child react to a change?

FOOTNOTES

[1]Burton L. White, *The First Three Years of Life* (New York: Prentice Hall Press, 1985), p. 151.

[2]*Ibid.*, p. 110.

[3]*Ibid.*, p. 151.

[4]Susan Byrne, "Nobody Home: The Erosion of the American Family," *Psychology Today* (May, 1977), 10:12, p. 44.

[5]*Ibid.*

[6]Sally Abrahms, "Full-Time Moms Develop Special Ties," *USA Today* (May 7, 1987), p. D4.

[7]Marilyn Fabe and Norma Wikler, *Up Against the Clock* (New York: Random House, 1979), p. 105.

[8]Gloria Norris and Jo Ann Miller, *The Working Mother's Complete Handbook* (New York: E. P. Dutton, 1979), p. 105.

[9]Patricia McCormack, "Kids Benefit from Working Mothers," *Los Angeles Times* (January 13, 1984), Section 5, Column 1, p. 28.

[10]Claudia Wallis, "Is Day Care Bad for Babies?" *Time* (June 22, 1987), 129:25, p. 63.

[11]Sandra Scarr, *Mother Care, Other Care* (New York: Basic Books, Inc., 1984), p. 19.

[12]Wallis, *op. cit.*, p. 63.

[13]*Families That Work: Children in a Changing World* (Washington, DC: National Academy Press, 1983), p. 311.

[14]*Ibid.*, p. viii.

[15]*Children of Working Parents: Experiences and Outcomes* (Washington, DC: National Academy Press, 1983), p. vii.

[16]*Ibid.*, p. 227

[17]Mary Battiata, "Centers Increase Risk of Childhood Disease,"

The Washington Post (July 6, 1983), p. A11.

[18]*Ibid.*

[19]Rich Spencer, "Children Whose Mothers Work Are Studied," *The Washington Post* (September 5, 1985), p. A15.

[20]Charles Babcock, "New Study Finds Children of Working Mothers Suffer in School," *The Washington Post* (June 6, 1983), p. A5.

[21]Sally Squires, "Students Do Better When Mother Works, Study Says," *The Washington Post* (August 24, 1986), p. A8.

[22]Battiata, *op. cit.*, p. 128.

[23]Dale Farran, "Now for the Bad News," *Parents* (September, 1982), p. 81.

[24]Alison Clarke-Stewart, "The Day-Care Child," *Parents* (September, 1982), p. 144.

[25]Farran, *op. cit.*, p. 81.

[26]Ralph E. Smith, editor, *The Subtle Revolution*, Washington, DC: The Urban Institute, 1979), p. 147.

[27]Barbara J. Berg, "Mothers Against Mothers," *The Washington Post* (January 3, 1986), p. B5.

[28]Carol Krucoff, "Mothers or Others," *The Washington Post* (December 18, 1985), p. 13.

[29]Sue Mittenthal, "Can You Work and Have a Happy, Healthy Child?" *Glamour* (August, 1985), 83:8, p. 32.

[30]Scarr, *op. cit.*, p. 184.

9.
Your Husband

I quite often finish leading a workshop and feel that I have gotten as much from the participants as I have given them. I recall a particularly profound comment from a young woman several years ago. She was a consultant who worked four days per week. Her husband, a government employee, also worked four days weekly. Their two preschool-age daughters spent the other three days in a day-care situation.

When they found the wife was pregnant with their first child, this couple sat down and figured out exactly how much money they would need each month. Next they discussed which work alternatives would allow them to earn this income, yet spend as much time with their children as possible. Neither one was happy with the prospect of full-time substitute child care. The part-time option meant professional sacrifices for both of them, but the arrangement has worked well for several years and they each feel the choice was best for the family.

At the close of the workshop, I asked if anyone had any last-minute thoughts and this woman raised her hand and said:

"I really feel I need to say something to every woman in this room. So many men, when confronted with the prospect of a working wife respond in attitude and/or words something like this, 'Sure, it's fine if you want to work, *provided* that everything continues to run smoothly at home (i.e., my life isn't disrupted at all). If you can do this without causing problems, sure, we could use the money!'

"*Don't* settle for this attitude! The children belong to both of you. Your home belongs to all of you. Each member is an integral part of the family. The responsibilities and joys are yours to share. Don't permit it to be any other way."

115

CHANGING EXPECTATIONS

What do men and women expect from each other? I suppose the answer is as varied as couples are. Some are quite happy pursuing the traditional roles of male breadwinner and female caretaker. A few switch roles and the vast majority are busy working out something in between.

One thing is certain: the times, they are a-changing! My parents were typical of their generation. My father drove off to work after breakfast and came home before dinner. My mother was left to a day of supervising and chauffeuring children, doing housework, and running errands. My father helped with certain household chores. He controlled the money and I suspect had the last word in most major decisions. He was interested in my sister's and my activities, and proud of our accomplishments. But it was my mother who took an active role in PTA, schoolwork, Brownies, piano and dance lessons, a myriad of sports, etc. In decisions regarding the home and the girls, I think my father usually deferred to my mother's judgment. My mother quit her job when she became pregnant with me, and it has never crossed her mind to return to the work force.

My own children will have much different memories. I'm not perceived as their primary caretaker. They are just as likely to scream "Dad" as "Mom" when waking up with a nightmare. We both volunteer in their schools and with their activities. They have seen both their mother and father perform most household chores. Name a day of the week, and they will tell you which parent will be home after school, or if they go to the sitter's house.

Our family is not unique. I see increasing numbers of men doing grocery shopping, taking turns in carpools, at children's lessons, at school, etc. When I organized a cooperative playgroup last year, two of the five parents (for a noon to 2:00 p.m. time period) were fathers. Not long ago, at a gathering of our friends including seven couples, we discovered that six of the seven men were responsible for getting children off to school or child care in the mornings.

I think things were easier thirty years ago (not necessarily better, but definitely easier). There is still a tremendous amount of confusion about male-female roles. The evidence suggests that philosophical pronouncements are not always validated by daily activities. Furthermore, what works for a childless couple in an apartment does not always succeed in the big house with a mortgage, a yard, two kids, a dog, etc.

In *Turning Points*, Ellen Goodman suggests that for many, changes in sex roles have created crises. The most common fear for both men and women is loss of the relationship. A woman in the workplace tends to develop a stronger sense of independence and wants this reflected at home. Her partner may inhibit changes the woman feels vital to her identity. Many women avoid pushing for change at home for fear of losing or damaging the relationship with their spouses. In addition, it's difficult to alter a pattern of caring and daily living that has been in existence over time.[1]

Goodman feels that this is the basis for the proliferation of superwomen. A superwoman justifies her employment by attempting to perform her traditional job as caretaker just as well as if she did not have a paid job. She often is reluctant or afraid to ask her husband to accept more responsibility at home. This is particularly true of nonprofessional women who are likely to bring home small paychecks.[2]

In 1983, the results of a ten-year national study about the changing roles of men and women were published in a book entitled *American Couples*. The researchers came to the following conclusions about couples, their relationships and their work:

- Working-class husbands are particularly vocal about assigning housework to wives.

- When husbands do a lot of housework, couples have greater conflict. The more work the man does, the more they fight about it.

- Men feel the "successful" partner should not have to do housework.

- Work and relationships are intertwined for women, and can be mutually enhancing.

- A working wife makes her husband more ambitious, and this competition is good to a certain extent.

- When both partners are work centered, the relationship goes on "automatic pilot" which may not be noticed until they hit turbulence.

- Women are more likely to put the relationship before their work.

- If at least one of the partners is not relationship centered, it is hard for the marriage to survive.[3]

The big choice is tied integrally to the topic of male-female roles, who is responsible for what and just what the partners expect from one another. Theresa, 27, of Reston, Virginia, is currently on maternity leave with her second child and does not want to return to her part-time job as a computer analyst. She has the financial freedom to stay home which she did not have with her older child, now 3 years old. She and her husband have been debating the issue throughout her leave period. Theresa's husband agreed that he did not want their two children in day care, but wanted her to find a way to work around the children.

> "This is the first time in our marriage that he's been the only breadwinner. So it's been a big adjustment. . . . I don't want it to be too much of a strain. I'd like to help, but this job I have now would just be too much.
>
> "He agrees with the children not being with a sitter. However, I don't think that he thinks it would be that difficult for me to work at home. They (her employer) offered to put the computer in the house. He thinks that sounds great. Well, last night I was here at 10:30 and hadn't done the dishes. At 11:00 I finally got a shower. How am I going to put in any kind of quality time? . . . He's getting to see my point. At first, he said, 'Well, you can get up in the morning early and work when they nap.' I just don't think men understand what goes on at home all day.
>
> "Sometimes we have friction. He says, 'This isn't the 1950s you know. You can't stay home and bake cookies all day.' . . . He wants to be supportive, but the money is just the bottom line."

Contrary to their expectations, many middle-age women have found themselves in the workplace by choice or by circumstance. The opposite is true of most young women today. They fully expect to combine career and family, only to find out that no one is going to make it easy for them and they may be taking on two full-time jobs. Men are not sure exactly how much responsibility belongs to them, but it is apparent that their lives probably will be different than their fathers'.

I recently read a 20-year-old book entitled *The Case for the Working Mother*. It was written by an editor-in-chief of a division of a large publisher. She was also a mother. While much of the book could be quite applicable today, I was appalled as I read some of the following excerpts dealing with the husband's role:

> "The double job is virtually impossible if your husband is against the idea. If he isn't all for it, forget it. . . . a husband's cooperation is crucial to the success or failure of the employed mother.[4]

"Yet even the most cooperative husband cannot be expected to take on extra household duties that interfere with his work-and-rest schedule. One man may actually enjoy helping out with cooking or marketing, but another will feel complete, out of character if cast in such a role.[5]

"Even if you are lucky enough to have the most marvelous housekeeper in the world, and a husband who does not mind pitching in now and then, the chief responsibilities are yours. Whether you actually carry out the details or not, it is still up to you to see that Dad's dinner jacket is home from the cleaner on time, that Mary's new dress is hemmed for the birthday party, that Billy keeps his dentist appointment, that the repairman fixes the oil burner. A woman is never not-a-woman, whether she works or not.[6]"

We've come a long . . . haven't we?

IDENTITY CRISIS

Parental guilt over the work choice usually is associated with women, but a recent study indicates that husbands may be sharing it as well. Historically, research has indicated that employed women enjoy better mental health than homemakers, but their husbands fare less well than husbands of homemakers.

Researchers at Rutgers University (Staines, Pottick and Fudge) looked for the cause of the phenomenon. The first possibility which was investigated was whether housework demands were greater on husbands of employed women. The study showed absolutely no evidence that these men spent a significant amount of increased time in housework. Other areas which were explored to no avail were attitude toward the spouse's employment and constraints upon geographic mobility.

The guilt factor which affected mental health turned out to be what the researchers termed "breadwinner adequacy."[7] Men felt guilty that they could not support their families alone. Just as women have difficulty sharing the child-rearing role, their husbands are resistant to sharing the breadwinning role. Husbands want to be good providers and many want to do it by themselves.

In theory, men accept and even approve of their wives working. The Roper Organization found in a nationwide survey that nine out of ten men approve of their wives earning paychecks.[8] However, in practice, dual-career families may have sparked identity crises in many men.

Many husbands of working wives grew up in families where

their mothers were the emotional caretakers and their fathers were the financial providers. Husbands who do not perceive themselves as breadwinners may feel they have no identities. Jane Hood, a University of New Mexico sociologist, finds that for professional men, the psychological cost associated with giving up a "husband-centered" family may be greater than the benefits of their wives' additional incomes.[9]

WHO CLEANS THE TOILETS?

Not many people claim to like housework. It's endless so you never have a sense of completion. There is no concrete measure of value attached to a sparkling sink or vacuumed rug. You probably are not overwhelmed with praise when you do it, yet it is readily visible if you do not do it.

When there is no time for housework, only a limited number of options exist:

- Cut down on the activities that interfere with housework.
- Reduce your standards.
- Be more efficient in your chores.
- Get assistance from somewhere, paid or unpaid.

How reliable are husbands as a source of unpaid household labor? One of the women I interviewed happily reported the following:

> "I don't feel like there's a lot of role playing between the two of us. If we both get home around the same time, the first person home starts dinner and the other one helps clean up. If there's laundry to be done, it's not, 'Why haven't you done this laundry?' — he does the laundry. From a task situation, he has certainly helped out."

Most households do not run quite so smoothly and freely. The "whoever has time, does it" approach would last about one week most places. Then it would be apparent that no one has time and that nothing is getting done. Someone must take the responsibility for doing or assigning the work. Usually it is the woman.

Available data suggests that men are doing more around the home than they have in the past, but the increase is negligible. Their expanded participation is found more in the area of child

care than household chores. Consider the following results of
time-use studies and surveys:

- A National Institute for Mental Health study conducted in
  1976 concluded that the average woman spends seven hours
  a day on housework, including 80 different tasks. Both men
  and women exaggerated how much work the husband did.[10]

- In a *Redbook* survey of readers, nine-tenths responded that
  husbands were taking on more domestic duties. However 89
  percent reported doing "more than half" to "almost all" of
  the work.[11]

- Only about one in ten husbands share housework. Homemakers spend eight hours, 42 minutes on house and family
  work; employed women spend five hours. Men and children
  combined spend one-and-a-half hours each day on
  housework.[12]

- The Institute for Social Research at the University of Michigan
  claims that husbands spend 14 hours a week on housework
  and child care, up three hours from ten years ago.[13]

- The Wellesley Center for Research on Women reports that
  42 percent of women want their husbands to help more with
  child care and 36 percent want more assistance with housework.
  The Center found these results surprising, considering how
  little men do.[14]

- Recent time-use studies indicate that women, employed or not,
  contribute 70 to 75 percent to housework. Spouse and children
  do the rest. The upper limit for men is approximately 20
  percent, unless the wife is incapacitated.[15]

- Employed women spend twice the time with their children
  as employed men and two-and-a-half times in household
  chores. For both sexes, large amounts of time at work are
  associated with increased levels of work-family conflict.[16]

There has been a slight decline in total number of hours
devoted to housework over this century. Some of this may be
attributable to labor-saving devices, but more is due to a general
decrease in standards of cleanliness.

The new machines altered the lives of American housewives,
but the time savings has not been all it was promised to be.
In the early part of this century, the average housewife logged
50 hours of unpaid work per week. Today, that figure remains
approximately the same; working women reduce the number
to a mere 35 hours per week.[17]

The labor-saving devices appeared at the same time the
labor pool was drying up. Between 1910 and 1920, the number
of households rose from 20.3 million to 24.4 million. Yet the

number of servants dropped from 1,851,000 to 1,411,000 in the same decade.[18] Subsequent years showed an even more marked decline in the face of restrictive immigration laws.

Women are still stuck with most of the drudgery and apparently accept it. There are no longer full-time servants to help share the load. Nevertheless, many women do all they can to fulfill multiple roles without inconveniencing men. They report more family disturbance about their work than the family does.[19]

Women's attitudes partially explain the husbands' lack of participation in housework. Some find it easier simply to do it than to nag their mates about it. Others do not choose to lower their standards and feel that only they can do it properly. Many resist giving up their "turf" and some still confuse their own identities with spotless homes and families. Whatever the reasons, the times have not changed as much as we would like to think.

CROWDED CALENDARS

Many of us live hectic, busy lives. Work, school, meetings, lessons, sports, church, volunteer activities; it never stops. Even vacations often are an endless whirl of travel and activity. Some of it can be blamed on the society in which we live, but most of it is a result of choice. I confess to being one of the worst offenders. My life is dictated by schedules which are created, for the most part, by me. I seem to have an aversion to white spaces on my calendar.

There are still 24 hours in a day and seven days each week. When too much is scheduled, something has to give. The first thing to be sacrificed normally is time for self, in terms of either rest or leisure activities. This often has unhappy consequences not only for the woman, but for her family as well. Crowded calendars certainly are also found in homes of unemployed women. Many employed women choose not to devote time to the same activities that homemakers do. However, there is an undeniable added burden when both adults commit large blocks of time to their paid jobs.

One-third of all workers complain that job and family life interfere with each other "somewhat" or "a lot." Men report that excessive workhours conflict with time they would like to spend with their families. Women's biggest concerns revolve around schedule conflicts. Nevertheless, workers still give basically positive assessments of marriage and family life.[20]

Certainly the one positive outcome of time constraints upon women has been increased involvement of fathers in their children's lives. One study of the role of the father in child development points to the following consequences for children with actively involved fathers:

- Strong sex-role development in both sons and daughters.
- Positive effects on self-esteem.
- Better academic performance.
- High scores on personality adjustment measures.
- Willingness to accept responsibility for actions.[21]

Children depend on a constant, caring adult to take care of them. When they can have equal confidence in both parents, regardless of work status, it benefits the children. Jane, 30, chose shift work which involved a crazy schedule for her and less time with her husband in order to avoid substitute care for their two children (introduced on p. 50). She admits that her children would like her home all of the time, but thinks that their relationship with their father is stronger because she is not always there.

> "They have to say goodbye to me at night before they go to bed and know that I'm not going to be there for them if they get sick. My husband has been real good and they've learned to rely on him as much as they would have on me."

ACTIVE VERSUS PASSIVE SUPPORT

Almost all of the women we spoke with, as well as most of my friends and colleagues, indicate that their husbands support them in their work choices. This is not really terribly surprising. The decision is so integral to both life goals and daily activities, that serious disagreement on the issue probably would cause a conflict which would either call for resolution or present a serious threat to the marriage.

Particularly for professional women, there seems to be little concern voiced by spouses about combining career and family responsibilities. There may, however, be a lack of support in the actual carrying out of those two jobs. According to Jessie Bernard in *The Future of Motherhood*, a basic requirement for employed mothers is choosing the right husband. Studies indicate that the cooperation of the husband is critical to successful integration of domestic and professional roles. Some of the characteristics of supportive husbands are:

- Less power and production oriented.
- In less traditionally male professions.
- More reflective.
- Intellectually oriented.
- Egalitarian in behavior and values.
- In more flexible occupations, e.g. academic, scientific.

These men are able to accept successful wives and show a willingness to be accommodating.[22]

There is a very big difference between active and passive support from spouses. Active involvement is evidenced by viewing both the decision and its consequences as a joint responsibility. Susan, 34, is on a leave of absence from a full-time job and doubts that she will return (introduced on p. 38).

> "When I took my leave of absence, it was to the point that I was going to walk out the door or do something. He (her husband) talked me into the leave to see how much was (due to) the job. He could see that a lot of my stress was because I wasn't doing what I felt I should be doing for the kids. . . I was just under total chaos all the time.
> ". . . It got too hard on them (the children). He could see what the job was doing to the family. He said, 'I would like us to sit down and figure out a way for us to pay the bills and pay for the house so you can stay home.' So we sat down and figured out what we could do. He was definitely supportive by that point."

Making the decision is one thing; living with it is another. If the choice results in problems, it needs to be reexamined. If things are working well, you still need ongoing affirmation of the decision. The daily family responsibilities need to be decided and agreed upon jointly, regardless of work status.

Dottie, 28, is a homemaker with two preschoolers (introduced on p. 95). Her husband is a real estate agent with a flexible schedule which allows him to be at home during the day frequently. He shares family responsibilities and supports Dottie totally in her decision to be at home with their children.

> "He's been very supportive and probably feels as strongly about a parent being at home full time as I do. I have certainly never felt any pressure from him that I bring in additional income.
> "He encourages me in the things I do at home and encourages me when we are really broke that my working is not a solution. I find myself saying, 'I've got to get a job,' and he says, 'No.' He encourages me in my decision.

"Also I see how seriously he takes his role as a primary breadwinner in order to make it possible for me to do this."

Passive support often is manifested in the attitude of the husband who wants his wife to be happy, but views the employment decision as hers to make. It is also hers to implement. He may be helpful in caring for children, doing household chores, etc., but the bottom-line responsibility is hers. Her decision should not interfere inordinately with his career.

Helen, 39, resides in a large Eastern city and is managing editor of a local women's magazine. She worked part time for many years after her children, now 9 and 5, were born. Her current job responsibilities demand a near full-time schedule. Helen's husband supports her decision to work and when possible, does carpool runs or cares for the children for an evening or weekend so she can go somewhere with friends. She believes, however, that the burden of juggling falls mostly to her:

"I'm still the one who's called on if anything happens. If I'm called that a child is sick, I'm the one who's expected to go pick the child up. My husband travels a great deal, so he's just not available a lot of the time. He often has to work weekends. He is supportive, but if I had a job that impinged a lot on our personal lives, something would have to give.

"I think when both parents work, one of their jobs has to be flexible. There has to be one person who can leave if need be."

NO SUPPORT

There is also a wide range of husbands who are not supportive of their wives' employment choices. The spouse may be intentionally uninvolved, and possibly unconcerned with the whole process. He may have a difference of opinion with his wife about the issue and actively try to change her mind. Worst of all, he may be openly antagonistic to her decision. As I pointed out earlier, this type of conflict usually does not last for long. One of the partners eventually accepts the other's point of view or the marriage is seriously threatened.

Once again, most of the resistance was offered by husbands facing a change. In some cases, it was when the wife returned to work after being a homemaker for years. In other instances, the wife suddenly decided she wanted to quit a job and be at home.

Diane, 40, shocked her husband when she quite suddenly returned to work after many years as a homemaker (introduced on p. 38). Her income has allowed them to enjoy many extras and her spouse is quite happy now that she has been working awhile. Initially, however, she feels that he had some reservations and felt threatened by her decision.

> "I think at the beginning, he wasn't real thrilled. He was a little bit leary of me leaving the girls and being out in the business world and meeting other people. But now he's a much happier person.
>
> "He was just a little nervous about me going to work. I think it's always safer for a man to think his wife is at home and is going to make these nice dinners every night and have things more comfortable for him.
>
> "You never know. This year, I'll be doing some traveling at work and going to a couple of locations. It's a hard step for a man who's had a wife at home for ten years."

Some men feel threatened by their wives return to the labor force; others are frightened when wives quit jobs. The primary concern is usually finances, and the husband's increased burden of being the sole support for the family. Some men may anticipate unfavorable changes in the marriage relationship or family dynamics.

Lynda, 39, worked through much of her older children's lives, now 16 and 11 (introduced on p. 88). After several miscarriages, when she became pregnant last year, she announced that she was leaving her secretarial job for good. She loves being at home with her infant son, but says that her husband was reluctant about the decision at first.

> "My husband was the hardest one (to convince). That $10,000 a year was really important to him. He doesn't see the stress that I felt. I guess I handled things well enough that it wasn't bothering him. It was the hardest for him to accept because he handles all the finances.
>
> "But when I said, 'This is the way it's going to be,' then he supported me. Now I think that he really likes me being at home. He's said I'm more relaxed, and that things go better and that I have more energy and time for everybody, and he likes that. The house is more ordered."

Occasionally, husbands initiate the change. Phyllis, 44, is married to a foreign service officer and they have relocated often during the course of their marriage (introduced on p. 82). Now that her only son is 16, Phyllis is deciding what to do with the rest of her life. She feels pressure, but not support from her spouse.

"In the early years, his support was stronger. He's certainly not kicking me out, but he lets me know that he thinks I ought to get some gainful employment. I don't know what he's worried about. The support could be better; not so much financially, though I think it's that for him, but more encouragement in helping me find what I want to do.

"He's very subtle about it. He doesn't talk about it. . . . Maybe I'm reading things into it that aren't there. He brings home (job) announcements from the State Department. . . . Yesterday morning he was looking through the classifieds and suddenly said, 'Bank tellers! There are lots of jobs for bank tellers!' I looked at him and said, 'So, for you or for me?' I thought, 'Why is he looking at jobs for bank tellers? I'm not a bank teller. He's not a bank teller.' I decided not even to ask. The pressure is there subtly. I'm certainly feeling it."

Raising a family takes an inordinate amount of time and effort. Working outside of the home also requires a commitment of time and energy, which varies depending upon the number of hours worked and the type of position held. If you are married, and your spouse is not supportive of your decision, it may prove to be an overwhelming obstacle, regardless of work choice.

EQUALITY

Is there such a thing as equality in the home? While many couples espouse jointly-shared home and family responsibilities, there is little evidence that this really exists to any great degree. Even in cases where husbands are highly supportive and cooperative, they are still viewed by both partners as "helpers." In most of the families with which I am familiar, women provide more of the child care, perform most of the domestic duties or hire substitutes, and are the ones who arrange the daily activities for their children.

There have been several hypotheses put forth explaining why action has not caught up with philosophy. Men are not used to the responsibilities and have no role models to follow. Because there are so few men in this role, there are no support systems of which men can take advantage. Men accept the idea but resist action because they have underlying doubts about taking on traditionally female tasks. Women's investment in the family is greater because of biological dictates; therefore, she will make sure that things work.

Whatever the reason(s), part of why men do not do more is because women allow them to do less. Several of the articles I read suggested ways in which women could get more "help." One listed several points which I thought might be useful in getting a six-year-old to clean his room, but did little to promote shared responsibility:

- Give up control.
- Don't be a martyr.
- Try a new vocabulary.
- Praise.
- Don't criticize when he helps.
- Don't treat him as if he were dumb.
- Give the information necessary to do the job.
- Know your man and give him a job he likes.[23]

Who, I wonder, does the jobs that no one likes?

I found the following approach from *The Working Mother's Complete Handbook* to be more palatable:

- Don't let him help when it's convenient; sharing requires sacrifice.
- Once he has taken on a responsibility, let him handle it his way.
- Agree on backup plans for emergencies and be prepared to implement them.
- Try to share tasks according to preference and convenience.
- Be willing to compromise.[24]

In Norway, a study was conducted of 16 couples who either shared one job or who both worked part time. Researchers found that the husbands and wives shared equally in the child care, but housework remained a female responsibility. Fathers reported that they felt closer to their children and understood them better. Mothers claimed to enjoy their children more when given a respite from full-time care. The children's interests apparently were better served by more equal attention from both parents. The study also revealed that marital relationships improved and there was better understanding of each other's joys and frustrations. The researchers concluded that work-sharing families experienced less stress and had better familial relationships.[25]

From a pragmatic standpoint, frequently there are obstacles to those who might desire egalitarian work-family status. Women get pregnant, have babies, and some breastfeed these babies. That means a recuperative period and possibly many months of being tied fairly closely to the child. In addition, statistics on earnings tell us that the husband is still likely to make more money than the wife, so absence from work does not have an identical impact upon family income. Finally, there may be an attitude problem. While it is considered acceptable for women to stay home with children or to work part time, men who do either are viewed suspiciously.

Only one of the women we interviewed stated that family and home responsibilities were jointly and equally shared with her husband. Arlene, 32, is a buyer who works full time (introduced on p. 96). She says that she and her spouse split home duties and time with the children.

"My husband is a major participant with these children. They were more his idea than mine almost. It's really a 50-50 operation. I don't come home and drive myself crazy and cook and clean and do all sorts of stuff. He does half of it and we have cleaning women.

"I don't think I'm married to the most typical type of man. . . . He takes them to day care everyday and picks them up. . . . If he weren't supportive, I couldn't be doing this. But I wouldn't have had the children if he hadn't promised up front to be supportive.

". . . Sometimes my husband says, 'I'll help you.' Even that phrase I resent. Why should he be helping me? Why is this house my responsibility? So we have discussions about that. He slips once in a while."

Changes in male-female roles have been dramatic over the past generation. For some, they have not been dramatic enough. For others, these same modifications have presented a threat to security and happiness. When it comes right down to it, who gets up with a sick child at night, who scrubs the kitchen floor, who plans the birthday parties, whose job gets priority, etc. are not matters to be dictated by society. They are issues that need to be worked out within the confines of each couple's relationship.

YOUR EQUATION

The issues you should consider and may want to include in your equation are the following:

- What do you expect from your husband regarding the big choice?
- Are you both comfortable with the roles you have now?

- How much time does your husband spend caring for your children?

- Which household responsibilities belong to him?

- Who is responsible for the planning necessary to keep the home running?

- Who is responsible for children's activities?

- Does your husband support you in your work choice?

- If so, would you describe it as active or passive support?

- If there is no support, how much of a conflict does this present for you?

- Is anything likely to change in the future?

FOOTNOTES

[1] Ellen Goodman, *Turning Points* (Garden City: Doubleday & Co., Inc., 1979), p. 57.

[2] *Ibid.*, p. 152.

[3] Philip Blumstein and Pepper Schwartz, *American Couples* (New York: William Morrow & Company, Inc., 1983), pp. 145-171.

[4] Dorothy Whyte Cotton, *The Case for the Working Mother* (New York: Stein & Day, 1965), p. 32.

[5] *Ibid.*, p. 120.

[6] *Ibid.*, pp. 151-152.

[7] Judy Mann, "Sharing the Load, Not the Guilt," *The Washington Post* (March 28,1986), p. B3.

[8] "Careers, Marriage, Children — New Poll," *U.S. News and World Report* (December 2, 1985), 99:23, p. 12.

[9] Amy Wilbur, "Working Women and Weak Men," *Science Digest* (July, 1986), 94:7, p. 21.

[10] Linda Lee, "Help! How Can I Get My Husband to Help Around the House?" *Redbook* (September, 1984), 163:5, p. 97.

[11] *Ibid.*

[12] Letty Cottin Pogrebin, *Family Politics* (New York: McGraw-Hill Book Co., 1983), p. 145.

[13] Marlys Harris, "The Three Career Live," *Money* (May, 1985), 14:5, p. 110.

[14] *Ibid.*

[15] Maxine L. Margolis, *Mothers and Such* (Berkeley: University of California Press, 1984), p. 177.

[16] Graham Staines and Joseph Pleck, *The Impact of Work Schedules on the Family* (Ann Arbor: The University of Michigan Press, 1983), p. 120.

[17] Ruth Schwartz Cowan, "Why I Love/Hate My Clothes Washer," *The Washington Post* (February 15, 1987), p. C3.

[18] *Ibid.*

[19]Pogrebin, *op. cit.,* p. 125.

[20]Staines, *op. cit.,* p. 120.

[21]Michael E. Lamb, *The Role of the Father in Child Development* (New York: John Wiley & Sons, 1976), pp. 23, 105, 109.

[22]Jessie Bernard, *The Future of Motherhood* (New York: The Dial Press, 1974), p. 162.

[23]Lee, *op. cit.,* p. 97

[24]Gloria Norris and Jo Ann Miller, *The Working Mother's Complete Handbook* (New York: E. P. Dutton, 1979), p. 113.

[25]Ross D. Parke, *Fathers* (Cambridge: Harvard University Press, 1981), p. 103.

10.
Your Relatives, Friends and Neighbors

Input from relatives, friends, and neighbors probably will not carry the same weight in your equation as the consideration of your children and spouse. Family members are usually the most influential of this group. You can choose your friends and you can discount or ignore your neighbors, but relatives can not be traded in for more cooperative models. In some instances, they are not easy to ignore either.

The encouragement or criticism you get from all of these various sources most likely leaves you with a general sense of support or a lack thereof. You may get extremely divergent input, for example, positive feedback from friends and business colleagues and constant criticism from family members.

Making a wise decision and having support from the "major players" in the drama will allow you to deal more easily with criticism even when it comes from people who care about you. Such disapproval may be borne from a genuine concern about you and your family. On the other hand, it may be due to the fact that you have made a decision which is contrary to what someone else has chosen or offends his or her sense of what is "right."

Support from these three groups can come in two forms. One is approval of your decision and reassurance that it is beneficial to you and your family. The other is concrete assistance in living with the results of your choice. This could take the form of financial assistance, child care relief, organized activity which frees up time for you, carpools, shared meals, etc.

Lack of support also takes various forms. If criticism or questioning comes from an individual with whom you have a close relationship, there may be open conflict until the difference is resolved. More frequently, the reaction seems to be an underlying feeling that this person does not approve of your decision, and it may make you uncomfortable. Some women choose to ignore the lack of approval with an attitude of, "This is my choice; I'm going to do what I think is best and it's none of their business; I don't care what they think!"

FAMILY TIES

It is very difficult *not* to care about our family's reaction to the big choice. Most of us grow up incorporating family values and seeking approval of family members, particularly parents. While this need for approval is not as apparent during the adult years, a remnant of it remains as long as the relationship exists. Disapproval of your choice often carries with it the implication that you have rejected part of what your parents considered important to pass along to you.

Jane, 30, works a night shift and considers her choice a result of economic circumstances (introduced on p. 50). She works hard to supplement her family's income and to arrange her work to have the least impact upon her family. The reaction she would like from her relatives is support and understanding, but she perceives neither:

> "I don't think they are very supportive. . . . I only have one brother who is married and they are financially very stable. She doesn't have to work. I think she understands (why I work).
>
> "My mom doesn't really enjoy the fact that I have to work, but I think she probably understands. They're not real sympathetic about it. Sometimes you wish they'd say, 'I really am proud of you for working so hard. I feel bad that you have to do it, but I'm glad that you're doing as much as you can.' Nothing like that has ever been said, which would be nice.
>
> ". . . Instead, it's 'Why don't you find a job with decent hours?' I think they think that if we had to we could make do without me working. We could, but we'd get further in debt, which I don't want to do.
>
> "It's always on my mind. Mom and I have never had the relationship that I want. I think I've always tried to do things that I think will please her or that I think will make her proud of me. I haven't come to something yet that will make her proud of me. . . . Maybe she is, but she's just not voicing her opinion."

All parents have dreams for their children and want the best for them. "What's best," of course, is open to interpretation and may be defined differently by the child and by the parent. There is also a significant difference between wanting the child to be happy and wanting the child to make the parent happy. Dreams can turn into expectations. Living up to other peoples' expectations is not an easy task.

Some of the women we interviewed gave some thought as to whether or not they were living their lives the way they were "supposed to" according to their parents. Susanna, 37, gave up her medical practice in order to "diffuse the stresses of life" (introduced on p. 39). She expressed a certain amount of doubt as to whether or not she was fulfilling her father's desires for her.

> "To a significant extent, they (her relatives) probably do (support me). I'll hear comments occasionally about, 'When are you going back to work,' or 'Do you plan to go back to work?'
>
> "My mother died years ago. I think in a way it may disappoint my father that I'm not using the years of training and the marvelous opportunities I've had professionally.
>
> ". . . I respect his opinions very much. He's a marvelous individual . . . and a very wise man. He's basically willing only to be involved if we ask him. He's never been strong about me returning to work . . . or made me feel unworthwhile at home.
>
> "I don't think his opinion is negative enough to sway me. . . . I respect his opinion and I've sought his advice on occasion, but in this instance, my husband and I both feel this is right and my father doesn't push it. So there's not a significant conflict at all."

A few working women stated that their "at-home" relatives were resentful that they were not available to take care of them, do things with them, etc. One part-timer saw her job as a welcome excuse for not bringing her children to her mother-in-law's home daily or going on lengthy shopping expeditions to which she was frequently invited. On the other hand, some working women wish they had more free time to spend with family members or to be available to relatives in need.

The extended family appears to be a thing of the past. If anyone lives with the nuclear family, it is generally a widowed parent. Fewer and fewer families have a large number of relatives living in the same town. In some areas, it is common not to have any family at all within "easy visiting" distance. The Washington metropolitan area where I live is a perfect example of this. Most people I know, including our family, do not have a relative outside the nuclear family within a sixty-mile radius. This means that most visits need to be planned and emergency assistance is more than a phone call away.

In those instances where relatives do live nearby, the most important support comes in the area of child-care relief. Family relationships seem to be preserved best when the relief is on a temporary or part-time basis. One full-time working woman whose daughter is in day care five days a week reports that the child rarely spends even three days a week there. An aunt or grandmother will often come and take her on a special outing. Her situation, however, is rather unique in the fact that she and her husband both have large families nearby and their children were the first born of their generation. Most of us are not fortunate enough to have hordes of doting relatives waiting in the wings to entertain our offspring.

Sometimes relatives simply agree to disagree. There is an obvious difference of opinion or choice, but it is ignored or accepted as such. There is no approval, but also no attempt to change the other. Gaylene, 30, is a homemaker and the mother of three children (introduced on p. 42). She feels strongly that preschoolers should have at-home moms. In her view, part-time employment is acceptable only when children have entered school and provided that the job does not disrupt family life. Her sister feels differently.

> "I could not go to work and leave my child with someone else, especially if they were sick or something. If you have a job, it's your responsibility and you have to leave the child. It just crushes my heart to think that child doesn't have the mother he needs.
>
> ". . . My one sister says that she'd go batty if she had to stay home. She's working, but that's her personality. My sister doesn't bother me at all. It has no effect on me. It just rolls right off my back when she says stuff."

GENERATION GAP

The term "generation gap" may be only a generation old, but the phenomenon has always existed. Adolescents all go through a period of examining and rejecting, to various degrees, the mores and values of their parents. As they settle into adulthood, former rebellious teens often end up looking like carbon copies of Mom and Dad. Regarding work and family issues, the generation gap has been apparent and has persisted on a national level. The majority of mothers today are not raising their children in the way their mothers raised them. For many, this has not been a choice. For those for whom it has been a choice, explaining the decision has led to some interesting confrontations.

When we asked the question, "Have you gotten support in your decision from relatives?" invariably the first family member the woman referred to was her mother. Almost all references to relatives were female family members. Rarely were men even mentioned, and if they were, their opinions were not perceived as strong convictions. Therefore, they were ascribed little importance.

Most women apparently feel that the decisions regarding how to raise the children fall primarily in their domain. Betty Friedan, in *The Second Stage*, claims that women seek to perpetuate the power that they have gotten traditionally through the home. They exercise this power over activities, the physical home and family life.[1] Decisions about the family and the home are the woman's "property." Therefore, women often are more concerned about "What would your mother think?" than "What would your husband think?" because your mother knows more about these things.

Many women's choices validated the choices their mothers had made. Homemakers felt that they had thrived on a secure childhood with an available mother and wanted their children to have the same. Some of the working women had working mothers (rarely during preschool years) and those women felt they had learned independence and a greater respect for their mothers' abilities from this role model.

However, in most cases, today's mother is not doing what her mother did. Where this decision involved a rejection of the role of full-time motherhood, the sentiments expressed fell along the following lines:

- "I don't want to be middle-aged with an empty nest and nothing to do."

- "I don't want to live my life through my husband and my children."

- "Life is too uncertain; I don't want to be left alone and unable to support myself."

- "Pouring so much energy and attention into the children is unhealthy for them."

- "Homemakers are perceived as dull and I don't want to be dull."

For a generation of women who did choose to make family and home a consuming priority, this is probably not the kind of feedback they expected nor wanted to hear from their grown daughters. These sentiments are rarely expressed so blatantly, and possibly never even verbalized. However, the decision to take a different road is a statement in and of itself.

For some, the different road has meant staying at home with children. Some of the most vehement supporters of mothers at home were women whose own mothers had worked when they were children. It is hard to distinguish what portion of their negative feelings is due to actual deficiencies in their upbringing and what is the result of being different in an age when most mothers were at home.

Phyllis, 44, has a teenager and is now beginning to turn her attention toward a career and what she is going to do with the rest of her life (introduced on p. 82). She has had no second thoughts about her decision to be a homemaker these past sixteen years. Her father died when she was an infant and her mother worked out of necessity.

"I did not work because of my past. I grew up as a latchkey kid way before it was as common as it is today. . . . Having been a child like that, I felt very strongly from early on that I wanted to be able to raise my child as I saw fit and be available to do the things I thought a mother should do.

". . . It also motivated me to become a teacher. My mother said teaching was the best profession for a woman, giving you those options to go back to it later on and to have vacations home with the kids. That made sense.

". . . I don't think Douglas even sees the issue. I've never been away enough for him to feel deprived, the way I missed having a mother. I noticed it when my mother would be home a couple of weeks and it would be so nice. I'm usually home for Douglas and the few days I'm not, it doesn't seem to bother him. He's perfectly happy to spend the afternoon alone."

Occasionally, the change in choice will manifest itself through several generations. Cindy, 32, is a human resources consultant for the Federal Government. She resides in Fairfax, Virginia with her husband and two children, ages 5 and 3. She has worked part time since having children. Her current schedule calls for four days a week in the office and out-of-state business trips. Cindy describes her mother as the "perfect mother," an excellent cook, seamstress, golfer, and bridge player. Their different beliefs about a mother's role has led to numerous confrontations.

"(I faced) a lot of resistance initially, especially from both of our mothers. I think my mother still has a concern. She was the product of a full-time working mother and she was an only child. She thought that there was nothing worse than that and thought I shouldn't work because of my kids and my husband. I would say she was probably as concerned about my husband as my kids, that he wasn't getting everything he should from a wife. . . . the traditional female role model for that era.

"I would say in the past five years as both parents have

watched the impact upon the kids and their fears have not been borne out (both of our kids seem to be very well adjusted). . . . They can't really point to my working as being a real problem. I think they are both concerned about my travel."

Some interesting distinctions were made between mothers and mothers-in-law. Not surprisingly, most women were more resentful of criticism or advice from a mother-in-law. Many simply took encouragement wherever it was available. One working mother reported large doses of understanding from her mother-in-law who had returned to work when her children entered school and "knew how hard things were." Her own mother who "plays golf all summer, skis all winter, and is worn out for a week when she cleans her refrigerator" just did not seem to understand.

Grandmothers are concerned with how their grandchildren are being raised. They also become alarmed if household operations are extremely different than their own way of doing things. Will everything turn out alright? Another frequent concern voiced by women's mothers is how the supermom regimen will affect their daughters.

Kathe, 37, operates her part-time accounting business around the lives of her husband and three children (introduced on p. 43). She gets different reactions from her mother and mother-in-law.

"Given their backgrounds, they've been pretty supportive. My mother basically would like me not to work. I think my mother-in-law, in her heart, feels that women shouldn't work. But she's also a real independent lady and says that's not what I would have done, but I know it's what you want and you're doing a good job.

"I think that my mother-in-law feels that I don't get everything done around here. I think that sometimes she can't believe what utter chaos the house is in. And when I do have free time, I spend it goofing off with the kids instead of cleaning up.

". . . My mother would rather see me at home with the kids, and out painting and riding. I think she would like to see me relaxing more but that's more out of concern for my well-being than the principle of it."

BIRDS OF A FEATHER

Very few women seem to get much negative feedback from friends regarding their work choices. Reactions generally range from support to indifference. There are several reasons for this. Unlike relatives, we have the ability to choose our friends and also more freedom to terminate relationships which are not rewarding or comfortable. Friendships are more likely to be endangered by issues regarding the personal relationship, not choices that one has made affecting her own career and family. Finally, you meet friends where you spend time. Therefore, working women tend to develop friendships at work. Mothers at home meet other homemakers in the neighborhood, through volunteer work, at children's activities, etc. People who are doing the same thing you are probably will be supportive of your decision.

Occasionally, women find themselves in a situation where they feel like the "odd person out." Laura, 30, lives in a community of Mormon friends (introduced on p. 54). She runs a preschool and gives private tutoring lessons. Most of her friends and acquaintances are homemakers.

> "My friends and neighbors are all at a different place and time right now than I am in that they are able to be at home all day with their children. So it is extremely hard for them to understand me packing up the kids and teaching preschool or tutoring or doing the things that I do. Other than socialization over the telephone and arranging time for our children to play together, I really couldn't say that I had their support. I don't think they understand it."

Others feel torn between two worlds. This is especially true in the case of a dramatic change in direction. One woman who had her first child after a career of nearly twenty years and then chose to stay home, got some raised eyebrows from her professional colleagues. Some of them openly questioned her choice and wondered if she had ruined her career. Another woman who reentered the work force after a long absence, reported some underlying resentment from old friends because she was no longer as available to them as she had been previously.

Some women successfully drift in and out of several diverse circles of friends. Susan, 36, of San Francisco, California, was the only female manager in a competitive computer business. When her first child was born over a year ago, she felt that she could not devote the necessary hours to her career and be able to have the time she wanted with her daughter. Susan chose to pursue an unfulfilled dream of developing her artistic talents on a commercial basis. She now runs a free-lance graphic arts business from her home. There is a real distinction in her mind between her friends, her former business colleagues, and the wives of her husband's business contacts.

"My close friends have been extremely supportive. I come from a work environment where there were no working mothers. You couldn't be a working mother with a 60-hour a week job. You can't do it. My other role is as a spouse to my husband in the banking community, which is very conservative. Almost all of the wives play tennis and do volunteer work. My group of friends are all doing their very best to survive and some of them are doing very well. So I don't really have any singular or clear type (of feedback)."

The image we have of ourselves is partially conceived in our own minds and partially created by others' statements about us. We are labeled not only by who we are, but also by what we do. Many women feel the need to be true to the picture they feel is expected by people who are close to them.

Barbara, 29, lives in Brookfield Center, Connecticut with her husband and daughter, age 2. She stayed home for nearly a year, going through an agonizing period of deciding when to return to work. She took one job which did not work out and is now working part time in her field of vocational rehabilitation. In retrospect, she is not sure of the primary motivating factor in her initial decision to go back to work.

"My friends and family were shocked that I was home for a year. I think I got less support when I was home full time. It wasn't expected of me because I was so career oriented. . . . It was a tremendous dilemma. I didn't know who I was going back to work for. So everyone could say, 'Oh look how she's managing, she works, she's raising a child, she's a homemaker, she's fabulous!' I just felt like there was a lot of respect along with all that. I didn't know if that was really what I wanted.

". . . My good friends expected me to be working. . . . Many of my friends in the neighborhood were working. When I first went back to work, I was living in a condominium and my friends knew me as a mother in my sweatpants all the time. When I would dress for work in a nice suit and with a briefcase, I would love to bump into my neighbors so that they could now see me not just as a mother, but also the professional woman. I would enjoy bumping into people so they could see the image that was really me. . . . The effect of their expectations was that I didn't know if I was going back for myself or for the image I wanted to live up to."

BACK TO THE FIFTIES

I grew up in a middle-class suburb of Baltimore in the 1950s and 1960s. We moved into our home when I was 3 years old and my parents sold that house the year I was married. Three of my bridesmaids were friends I had met in the first grade. We still see each other although none of us lives in the same state. Most of the families on the block also lived there for twenty years. Rarely were homes put up for sale. Neighbors were important and they were permanent.

The neighborhood was the first place a child made friends. There were children in most of the houses in our block and mothers in all of them. I never met a child who was cared for in someone else's home and no one knew what a day-care center was. Sometimes, as in our home, there was also a grandparent. The kids in the neighborhood spent hours at a time playing outside. No one locked their doors during the day and parents did not worry about child abduction. As we got older, our boundaries expanded, and we walked as many as ten blocks to play with friends whom we had met at school.

Neighborhoods resembling the one of my childhood can still be found. However, except in some parts of the country, they tend to be the exception, not the rule. I visited a neighborhood in York, Pennsylvania, that fits the bill. It is a fairly new development spanning a several-block area. There are more Big Wheels than cars and lots of children everywhere. Many of the families' social lives seem to revolve around neighborhood activities. There are Bible studies, game and card clubs, book clubs, sports activities, children's playgroups, and events for couples. I was told that there were three mothers in the entire development who worked full time.

Pat, 35, is a homemaker with two children and a third on the way. She teaches mathematics at the college level, less than ten hours per week. She considers herself and most of her neighbors fortunate in that they do have a choice of whether or not to work.

"My image of a homemaker is colored by this neighborhood and it does not necessarily mean household drudgery, nor even caring for your children full time. People use nursery schools a lot; some have housekeepers. . . . I feel that we have freedom to choose what we want to do. Some choose to work part time in order to make their lives more interesting.

"Even the people who stay home full time are involved in something that they want to do, whether they are paid for it or not. It may be volunteer activities, the Junior League, Young Women's Club, the PTA. When I am home full time, I am busy with a lot of things around here. I have fun doing things with people in the neighborhood and I feel their support. When I teach, I also feel they think that's wonderful, but it's because I don't work that much."

Around the corner from Pat lives Diane, 37, a medical technologist who increased her part-time schedule to full time this past year (introduced on p. 72). Her main priority this year has been learning to juggle her two roles successfully. The reaction from her neighbors to her choice can be summed up as sympathy, not support.

"Rather than support, they get this pained look on their faces and say things like, 'Gosh, you just put in incredible hours. You poor dear!' And quite frankly, some days I do feel like a poor dear. But I can't draw support from that. They have a different perspective being at home all day.

"That's the physical part of my work. What I do they find interesting. . . . They ask me questions (about medicine or the hospital). . . . Some of the same people that I know have voiced distress that I work so much or work full time, at the same time think that what I do is interesting and exciting.

". . . When I worked part time, I could participate in a lot of the neighborhood activities. I do feel a little out of it now, but not left out really. People know I work full time and have made the choice not to invite me because a lot of things I simply can't make. Even on weekends we've been too tired or doing things here. I keep thinking, maybe in error, that as the children get a little older and I master this hectic schedule and working full time, that things will improve. I do miss the contact and you bond with your friends."

NOBODY'S HOME

The scene is different today in most neighborhoods across the country. A couple of years ago, United Parcel Service discontinued its practice of having neighbors sign for packages when the recipient was not home. No one else was home either. Telemarketing firms load up their staffs at dinner hour, the most certain time to find someone to answer the telephone. Many activities once scheduled for after-school hours have switched to evenings or weekends.

It is difficult to make predictions about where you would find neighborhoods with a large number of mothers at home. Urban and suburban areas have a larger percentage of working mothers than rural areas or small towns and cities. In some communities, certain developments have a reputation for having a lot of at-home mothers. Many times the school districts dictate where families with children live.

My own observations of the area in which I live allow me to draw two conclusions. Developments of new homes and/

or moderately priced homes attract young families. Families with young children are the most likely to have mothers who are unemployed.

In my immediate neighborhood, there are few children and only two homemakers, to my knowledge. As a working mother, the lack of neighbors at home during the day does not affect me. I regret that my children do not have a large neighborhood "gang" of pals with whom to play. Last Halloween, I opened my door seven times for the neighborhood ghosts and goblins. Less than two miles away, a friend of mine reported that she had to turn off the lights and hide after she ran out of candy. Her estimate of her total number of trick-or-treaters to that point was 200!

Cora, 32, is a homemaker with two daughters, ages 4 and 8 months. She assists her husband with his dental practice, but does most of the work at home. She recently moved from my neighborhood to a new home just a couple of miles away. I asked her how she had felt at home in a deserted neighborhood.

"I don't think any neighborhood would have an effect on my decision to stay home. I knew I wanted to be home with my kids. . . . It just makes it less fun in a neighborhood where there aren't people home. One of the things that women with kids have is a certain amount of frustration at being in with them all day. I always walked up and down the street and rarely bumped into anybody.

"I think you just like to feed off each other, people who are doing the same thing. . . . We've taken a couple walks (in the new neighborhood) and I don't see anybody. I'm afraid this isn't going to be a good neighborhood to find people either.

". . . It just adds to the complications of being in a suburban neighborhood. You have to arrange visits (for children), get in the car, go pick them up. And with an infant, I have to work things around her schedule and drag her along."

Most of the working mothers felt that the neighborhood had little influence upon their lives or their decisions regarding work. They did not get much support from neighbors and did not particularly care. Some working mothers do rely on help from homemakers for emergency child care or transportation assistance. One mother of seven jokingly reported that she was the most popular woman in the neighborhood and that her name was on half of the emergency cards at the local school. Other homemakers resent being asked to fill in for mothers who have "abdicated their responsibilities."

Theresa, 27, is enjoying her maternity leave and being at home for the first time after the birth of her second child (introduced on p. 117). She sees the "war between women" being played out in her neighborhood.

> "There are not many mothers that stay home in this neighborhood. The ones that do, you feel like you get support from. The people who work, you feel like they're thinking, 'Gosh, what do you do all day? You can do more with your life!' People don't think that being home with children is enough. It's rewarding and I'm quite content.
>
> "My neighbor next door says, 'When are you going back to work? Don't you miss being with people and going out to lunch and getting dressed up and bringing in the money?' The whole thing sounds so flowery until you do it. Well, I think it's the pits. I don't know how women stay sane and do it."

In some neighborhoods, two separate cultures seem to survive and thrive. My husband and I were childless and both working full time when we bought our first house. Five days a week, I left at seven in the morning and returned at six in the evening. We had only a few friends in the neighborhood and they too, were working, childless couples.

My son was born in the month of March and I took advantage of the beautiful spring weather to take many walks pushing the baby carriage. I discovered a whole new neighborhood. Babies attract friendly people. I met scores of women with small children. (We lived in a new development of moderately priced homes.) I spent time at tot lots, in the baby pool and joined two babysitting cooperatives. It was an entire new world I had not even known about as a working woman.

Relatives, friends, and neighbors are interesting, if nothing else! Feeling at ease with a work choice which your children, spouse and you agree is best is an accomplishment. Expecting this decision to delight all of your relatives, friends, and neighbors is probably an impossibility!

YOUR EQUATION

The issues you should consider and may want to include in the "relatives, friends and neighbors" part of your equation are the following:

- Do your family members approve of your choice?

- Do you get tangible assistance in addition to positive feedback?

- If there is criticism, does it come from someone you can easily avoid?

- If there is disapproval, does it cause a dangerous level of ongoing conflict?

- Are you influenced greatly by others' expectations of you? If so, do you feel you are fulfilling them?

- Are you following in your mother's footsteps or taking another path?

- What does your mother think?

- Have most of your friends made the same choice you have?

- Do your friends form a support base for you?

- Are you living up to your image? Do you care?

- Are you the norm or the exception in your neighborhood?

- Is your neighborhood a support base for you?

FOOTNOTE

[1]Betty Friedan, *The Second Stage* (New York: Summit Books, 1981), p. 57.

11.
Society

It is difficult to define just who or what society is. Do women receive support from society in the decision to work or not while raising a family? Most of the responses I got were very strongly negative. Based upon the explanations of their feelings, I perceived that women think of society in one or more of the following ways:

- Media portrayal of women and families.
- A generalized consensus of opinion gleaned from conversations with and/or observations of others.
- Lawmakers and political philosophies.
- Institutions.
- Organizations speaking to these work-family issues, primarily feminists and conservative "pro-family" groups.

MEDIA

There are two commercials which I particularly detest. I dare not mention the products, but I bet you will recognize them. The worst, in my opinion, is a perfume advertisement where "Superwoman" slinks about being praised for bringing home the bacon and frying it too. This "new" woman can do it all (very easily and looking great all the time) needs a "new" perfume. Thankfully, it has not been on the air for some time now. My blood pressure soared each time I watched it.

The other commercial portrays the woman who spends her day in an evening gown lightly dusting the beautifully polished furniture. I keep hoping a disheveled four-year-old will come bursting in and run across the table top with muddy shoes. I wonder if she wears the same outfit to scrub her kitchen floor?

146

The hard work that is involved in what we do is rarely portrayed.

Men are conspicuously absent from many commercials. When they are seen, they frequently are smiling, silent, supportive men, happy that their wives have done a good job and wisely chosen the advertised product. Worse, if they are involved in performing a household task, they appear incompetent, implying, I assume, that the job needs a woman. They are usually popping a frozen prepared food in the oven or toaster, assuring the children that Mom will be back soon. Occasionally, men get to look disgusted, if their wives leave a "ring around the collar" or do some similar unthinkable act.

Another phenomenon is occurring in the media. The homemaker is vanishing. There are fewer magazines and news articles addressed to women at home. Television programs are almost devoid of young homemakers. Thirty years ago, career women were nonexistent. In the few programs portraying women who worked (Our Miss Brooks, Susie) they certainly did not have a husband or children. Now it is difficult for homemakers to find stories or characters with which to identify.

Television, because of the visual dimension, influences our perceptions more than radio or printed media. Undoubtedly, television is the worst offender in offering an unrealistic portrayal of work and family issues. The Commission of Working Women conducted a recent study of entertainment programs on network television. The purpose was to determine how everyday realities were depicted. They wanted to see how these shows portrayed child care problems, family budgets, distribution of household chores and women with multiple responsibilities.

The Commission concluded that these realities are nearly invisible. Money problems are rarely mentioned, child care is never a problem, and working women do not appear harried or tired. Children of working parents are either old enough to be self-reliant or are cared for by live-in help or loving relatives. Day-care centers do not exist and there are no latchkey children.[1]

The study also revealed that the families portrayed on television do not represent an accurate sample statistically. Most television children live with single parents. One-half are wealthy or upper-middle class. None of the single mothers portrayed are working class or poor. More than half of the children live with single fathers, who experience no great difficulties. In reality, 90 percent of single parents are mothers with an average annual income under $9,000.[2]

Most of us recognize the fact that television does not duplicate what we see around us everyday. At the very least, however, we get a subconscious message that says women should have careers, we should do it all easily and any problem that comes along can be solved with 30 minutes.

MATERIALISM

A popular rock song tells us that we're living in a material world, and few of us would disagree. Materialism has a rather nasty connotation to many people, of selfishness and misplaced priorities. Most of my acquaintances would not be proud to stand up and boast that they were materialistic. Maybe I just do not know enough hard-core yuppies.

Having things certainly is not wrong. We all need food, clothing, and shelter. However, people perceive and define "needs" in various ways. Where do we cross the boundaries from needs to desires to excessiveness? And is this a matter which needs to be explained and justified?

Many working women freely admit that the major purpose of their employment is to provide luxuries for the family. It could be family vacations, a bigger house, private school, or nicer clothes for the children. They feel that they should have as much of a right to work for these things as the women who use their paychecks for groceries and utility bills.

Some women, primarily homemakers, disagree. They feel as though working women have forsaken their children in the interest of things. They blame materialism as a motivating factor in many women's choices to work. Society is seen as encouraging this urge to have more, with no limit in sight. Below are comments from two homemakers on this subject:

> "We need to lower the American wants, of having two cars and a trip every year. They have to cut somewhere. Even the necessities cost so much. We have worked ourselves into this (predicament) from wanting and expecting so much in life. Everyone in America wants to keep up with the Joneses so they have to go out and have two paychecks in order to have the income to (provide things) to meet these desires that are important to them."

> "A lot of women use money as an excuse to feel they have to go back to work. I think we live in a very materialistic society. Many women feel they have to go back to work because they can't afford not to. In reality, they probably could stay at home and still do just fine, but maybe not have as much as they do have.
> "This is a problem society has placed on people because we are so materialistic. People always feel they have to have more than they do. . . . A child doesn't care if he lives in a

$40,000 house or a $140,000 house. He doesn't comprehend it.
It's important to the parents."

Once again, the judgments were not aimed at single parents
or poor families. It was acceptable to go to work if it kept your
family off the welfare rolls. It was not acceptable to deprive
children of a mother's attention for a trip to Florida, private
school or designer clothes.

Oddly enough, none of the negative feelings seemed to be
directed at the materialism, only working mothers joining in
on it. Edie, 44, lives in a wealthy community in Texas (introduced
on p. 81). She now works full time, but states that her salary
is not needed by the family. Her return to the work force occurred
when her youngest children reached the teenage years. She admits
a prejudice against women she sees who are working when their
children are small.

"Some of the young women who are going to work full
time, especially with young children; I don't exactly like what
I see. We live in a very affluent neighborhood here. I'm probably
not seeing the ones who are really struggling to make ends meet.
I'm beginning to see the Mercedes with the car seat and I feel
like sometimes they have given up some of what I feel are
important things in life for the materialistic things."

A desire to keep up with the Joneses is not limited to the
parents. Anyone with teenagers knows how important it is for
their children to be, look, and act like their peers and to have
what "everyone else" has. The pressure is on the kids, and it
is transferred to the parents.

I am embarrassed to admit that I bought my daughter a
pair of jelly shoes. I think they are unsafe to walk in and probably
bad for her feet. After months of resisting, I finally gave in.
I have confined her to the house when she is wearing them.
She puts them on whenever she can and struts around like a
movie queen. My only consolation is that they are cheap. I
am already working on arguments for why my son will not
need his own car a few years from now.

Even young children are able to make the connection
between Mom working and what her paycheck can buy. Alice,
32, is a homemaker who occasionally considers returning to
work (introduced on p. 60). She relates an interesting
conversation with her son, age 7:

"Derek has a little friend whose mother works full time and
this little boy has every toy imaginable and we always joke about

it. We got into a discussion about the fact that often his mom
is away (on a trip) and she brings back a toy. I asked Derek
if that was okay, and he said, 'Yes, that was fine.' Then I asked
him, 'Should I do that?' and he thought for a while and answered,
'Yes, I should.' That's just the stage he's at. They may not like
me around all the time, but I think it will be good for them
in the end.''

A NATIONAL DISGRACE

The United States is one of the few advanced countries with
absolutely no national policy regarding work and family issues.
There is no national initiative supporting parental leave, flexible
work arrangements, or quality day care. Our nation spends less
on child-care programs today than it did ten years ago.[3]

It was in 1971 that Richard Nixon vetoed a comprehensive
child-care program passed by Congress, stating that he refused
to put the Government's "vast moral authority" behind
"communal" approaches to child rearing.[4] There has been
relatively little Congressional activity in the last two decades
regarding work and family issues. Some presidential hopefuls
are espousing programs such as child-care subsidies for the
working poor, tax incentives for businesses to provide day care,
and information and referral networks. Meanwhile, the Reagan
Administration has cut federal funding for direct day-care
subsidies for low and middle income families by 28 percent.[5]

Sheila Kamerman, of Columbia University, has conducted
extensive research on worldwide maternity policies. Seventy-five
countries, including many developing nations and every
industrialized country except the United States, provide some
type of parental leave benefit. All but 16 have some sort of
national health insurance or sickness benefits. Among the
industrialized countries, the minimum paid leave is 12 weeks.[6]

One-third of female workers in our country have no health
insurance. The vast majority of this percentage are part-time
and young workers, who are quite likely to become pregnant.
Short-term leave of three months or less is available to most
workers. Paid leaves generally fall under disability overage. Only
20 percent have the option to expand their time off with unpaid
leave.[7]

The problems are not confined to inadequate maternity
leave. There are not enough flexible working arrangements to
permit parents to perform their two jobs and still take part
in school and community activities. Inadequate child care is
a concern, particularly for older children and infants. Corporate
benefits are still tailored to the one-earner family.

These stresses are taking their toll on American workers. A Boston University research project followed the lives of 651 employees of an unidentified company for one year. Interviews with employees showed that the main reason they got depressed at work was due to the strain of holding a job and raising a family at the same time. One-third of the working parents spent part of the day worrying a great deal about their children. The researchers concluded that the employees had done everything possible to ease the strain of work-family conflict and it was up to the corporation to take some action.[8]

It is curious that while work and family issues are so important and affect such a large segment of the population, proposed solutions get relatively little media coverage and almost no legislative action. What most people probably remember from the White House Conference on Families in 1981 was fighting between the representatives, arguments about the definition of the family, and focus on the Equal Rights Amendment, homosexuality, and abortion. Does anyone remember that the two most strongly supported resolutions were:

- Policies that enable persons to hold jobs while maintaining a strong family life, including flexible work arrangements, leave policies, and dependent care options (passed 569-21);

- Development of alternative forms of quality child care, both home and center based (passed 547-44)?[9]

Only one major piece of legislation has addressed these issues in the subsequent seven years, The Family and Medical Leave Act. This bill has had various names and has been before Congress for two years now. Introduced originally by Congresswoman Pat Schroeder (Democrat-Colorado), disability and parental leave would be sex neutral. Employees temporarily unable to work would be guaranteed 25 weeks of disability leave with health insurance and other benefits continued through the leave period.

Parental leave of a minimum of 18 weeks would be mandated for any parent choosing to stay home with a newborn, newly adopted, or seriously ill child. Under certain conditions, the parent would be allowed to return to work on a reduced schedule for an additional period of time. Benefits would be continued during this period. The bill also calls for the establishment of a commission to submit recommendations within two years for implementing a national paid leave policy.[10]

Employers with fewer than 15 workers would be exempt from the law. Employees would be required to work three consecutive months, or 500 hours, before they are eligible to apply for the leave. Despite the fact that the leave is unpaid, the bill still has received incredible opposition from the U.S. Chamber of Congress, small businesses and many professional organizations.

When the bill nearly passed the House last year, approximately 150 companies and trade associations joined forces to lobby against it. They formed Concerned Alliance of Responsible Employers (CARE) and were effective in slowing the bill. Now they have vowed to fight other "mandated benefits" bills as they are introduced.[11]

Just recently, other initiatives have been launched on the Hill. Legislation was introduced in the House of Representatives to establish a national clearinghouse for information on child-care services. A Senate subcommittee is holding hearings on the shortage of quality day care.

The U.S. Supreme Court earlier this year upheld a California law granting four months of unpaid maternity leave with job reinstatement rights. Thirty states are working on bills dealing with child care and parental leave. Thus far, however, there is far more talk than action across the country.

Almost all of the women we interviewed felt little or no support from society in their choices. Homemakers complained primarily about lack of esteem and an economic system which drives women to the workplace and ignores the value of labor in the home. Working women were angry that businesses and institutions did little to accommodate their work schedules. One part-timer felt that her group had the most "fragile super-structure" with double expectations and still no support.

Marilyn, 47, lives in Springfield, Virginia and juggles three part-time jobs as a bookkeeper, word processor, and administrative consultant. Her husband works for a nonprofit youth ministry and they live a hectic, fast-paced life with three active children, ages 10 to 15. Marilyn feels little support from society and does not believe that it is likely to increase as long as family life is not a priority of society.

> "If society placed a higher value on commitment to family and to standards that enhanced the family, then society could turn around and support women following through on their particular choices of career, and still maintaining family well. Right now, society polarizes all those things and does not know how to commit to family. Therefore, women don't have the freedom to make choices."

THE REST OF THE WORLD

What type of supports are other countries lending their citizens? When you think of advanced social programs, the first country to come to mind generally is Sweden, with its extensive social welfare system. They have free maternity and child health services, day-care centers and allowances for children and housing. The country is committed to full employment and equality of the sexes. Nonworking women subject their families to a tax penalty.[12]

Legislation in 1975 authorized shorter working hours for parents of young children and expanded preschool child-care programs. The Parental Insurance Scheme provides nine months leave with 90 percent of salary and pension security after the birth of a child. Parents may also take up to 60 paid days of leave to stay home with a sick child. Additional legislation passed in 1979 provides job-protected unpaid leave for either parent until the child reaches 18 months of age. Either parent has the right to a six-hour workday with income supplements until the child's eighth birthday.[13]

I was surprised to learn that Hungary has even more extensive statutory social benefits. The country supports the homemaker role for mothers of young children. Each mother receives a lump-sum cash, maternity benefit equal to one month's wages following the birth of a child to mitigate the costs of child-bearing. It is contingent upon parental care.[14]

Maternity leave entails five months of full wages. There is a flat-rate cash grant for child-care allowance and unpaid leave from work until the child's third birthday. The women maintains seniority, pension rights, and full job security. At age three, the child enters a national preschool program.[15]

Hungary's policy was originally conceived for labor market reasons. It was instituted as an incentive for unskilled women to withdraw from the labor force due to a labor surplus and inadequate day care. In 1974, a pronatalist movement instituted higher grants for second and third children. Eighty percent of Hungary's female workers use this benefit and the full leave is taken by one-third of mothers. More than half take leave of 24 months.[16]

Hungary has additional benefits which aid working parents. There is paid sick leave for employed women or sole male parents to take care of ailing children. Housing priorities are given to families with three or more children. Paid personal leaves are given to parents of children under 14 in the following increments: two days for one child, five days for two children, and nine days for three or more. There is also a family allowance which is a universal flat-rate cash grant to supplement the income of families raising children.[17]

The Federal Republic of Germany also has a national policy which supports the family. There are housing and child allowances as well as comprehensive health services. A cash allowance to parents in increasing amounts for subsequent children is designed to encourage fertility. Entitlements are available for children until age 18, or until age 27 if the young adult is enrolled in a university. In addition, there is a cash benefit paid on the birth of each child and a paid maternity leave for seven-and-a-half months.[18]

The U.S.S.R. has a national system of day care which services 13 million children. It dates back to the Russian Revolution. There is still a shortage of child care. Infants as young as two months old are accepted, but most mothers do not enroll their children until age 3. However, women are given four months of paid maternity leave and may take leave at 25 percent of salary until the child's first birthday. There is no paternity leave. Homes which have available grandparents to serve as babysitters are the last to be assigned to the nursery schools.[19]

Mothers in France may take 16 weeks of maternity leave at 84 percent of their salaries. There are state-run centers called crèches which service 79,000 children. The crèches are open 11 hours per day and the daily cost ranges from $3 to $18. The government also offers subsidies of up to $340 per month to parents who choose in-home help.[20]

Nearly one-fourth of Jewish youngsters under the age of four in Israel attend one of the 900 subsidized day-care centers and there is still a dire shortage of care available. The centers charge between $27 and $90 per month according to family income. After childbirth, mothers are entitled to 12 weeks of paid leave and 40 weeks of unpaid leave.[21]

The list goes on. One comparative study concluded that our country has a "do nothing" approach. Cash subsidies are available to low-income single mothers under the Aid to Families with Dependent Children program. This support, however, is based upon labor market withdrawal. We have no policy for low-income, two-parent families. We have no labor market policy. We have no family policy.

Sheila Kamerman found that the United States ranks low or last on much child-care provision and on all family social benefits.[22] It seems unbelievable that these issues can continue to be ignored in the face of skyrocketing female labor force participation rates and the obvious strain imposed upon working mothers, children, and families.

The former Secretary of Labor, William Brock, agrees. He is quoted as saying the following:

> "It's just incredible that we have seen the feminization of the work force with no more adaptation than we have had. It's a problem of sufficient magnitude that everybody is going to have to play a role: families, individuals, businesses, local government, state government. . . . The family is under a great deal of stress. We have to make sure we aren't part of the problem."[23]

In March, 1987, the Department of Labor sponsored a conference, which I attended, entitled Work and Family. The issues and the rhetoric were the same that I have been hearing for a decade. The exciting development was that the issues are finally being recognized by those in positions to effect change. The conference drew over one thousand participants from across the entire country. Many of the speakers and attendees were important names from business, government, and labor groups. While there is certainly no consensus on the solutions, at least the problems are now widely recognized.

SOCIETY'S MANDATE

Hopefully, the push is beginning for a national policy to aid working families. There appears to be a broader base of support now. Many divergent groups, women's organizations, religious groups, advocates for children, are at least agreeing that something needs to be done.

Some see the solution through economic means. Jeanne Mager Stellman, author of *Women's Work, Women's Health,* calls for a national task force to reevaluate the economic status of women at home and on the job. She feels that only a national economic program will eliminate poverty of large numbers of women and the economic exploitation of homemakers. The program would include on-the-job training for women with unmarketable skills, a full-employment economy so women would not be viewed as surplus labor and tax structure changes to benefit workers raising families.[24]

Others believe that economics are only a small part of the problem. Businesses must become more responsive to workers' needs. Institutions need to recognize that families no longer can be stereotyped and that services to these families must be diverse and appropriate. Perhaps most difficult, attitudes need to change before any substantive progress can be made.

I asked the women we interviewed, "What could society

do to make this choice easier for women?" The responses were comprehensive and extremely united. There was a real sense of need for changes to make things easier for all mothers. In addition, there was a recognition that change was necessary for the good of society, not just for the benefit of those directly affected. The "national agenda" they laid out for me follows:

Child Care

- Should be available near or on the work site.
- Make child care assistance part of the income package.
- Develop a supply of child-care workers.
- Pay child-care workers more money.
- Subsidize child care for low-income families.
- Providers should take children to school and outside activities.
- More options for child care should be available.
- Greater flexibility in programs and hours for part-time or shift workers.
- Better quality care, not just babysitting.

Alternative Work Patterns

- More part-time, flexitime, and job-sharing arrangements.
- Make flexible options available to men and women.
- Businesses need to change the rigid picture of what it means to accomplish tasks.

Maternity (Parental) Leave

- Guaranteed job security.
- Longer leave time.
- Uniform core time of paid leave with the option to extend with unpaid leave.
- Continued benefits during leave period.

Businesses

- More family-oriented work policies.
- Acknowledge that family welfare is partially a corporate responsibility.
- More flexible hours of operation for service industries and medical professionals.
- Relax nepotism policies.
- Spousal employment placement with corporate transfers.

Employee Benefits

- Gear toward diverse types of families.
- Increased flexible benefits programs.
- Sick leave available to care for dependent children who are ill.
- More personal leave or vacation time.

Equal Employment Opportunity

- End discrimination in the workplace in terms of jobs and pay so that women can afford the help they need.

Economy

- "Fix" the economy so two incomes are not necessary.
- Bring prices under control.
- Grant tax benefits and economic security to homemakers.
- End tax penalties against married couples who work.

Schools

- Schedule more activities in evening or early morning hours.
- Year-round school.
- After-school child-care programs in the public schools.
- Consider parents' time when assigning homework, asking for baked goods, sewn costumes, etc.

Television Programming

- More education shows.
- Take off the "junk."

Community Activities

- Increased use of recreational facilities after school and during vacations.
- Establishment of networking systems for parents to help each other in exchanging child care, car rides, etc.
- Referral system to locate mothers who want to be home with their children who might provide care for other children.

Men

- Change attitudes to recognize that home and family should be mutual responsibilities.
- Support, not ridicule, for participation in family life.

- Allow men a more leisurely career.

Advocate Choice for All Women

- Sanction either choice.
- "Extremist" groups should relax.
- Do not equate productivity with a paycheck.
- Do not distribute guilt to anyone.
- Do not ask women to explain or justify their choices.
- Educate young women and teach respect for the career of motherhood.
- Change attitudes toward working women.
- Give positive feedback and status to homemakers.

Finally, recognize that this is society's problem. Then we will be motivated to jointly seek solutions in lieu of individually struggling with these issues.

I think that most of these suggestions are good, but I do not agree with all of them. For example, I would be opposed to year-round school. While it might accommodate the needs of working parents, I do not think it is in the best interests of children. However, there were so many items on which so many women agreed, that it's amazing to me that we have been unable to effect more social change.

CORPORATE RESPONSIBILITY

If the Government has done little to address the problem, the majority of American businesses have not responded any more enthusiastically. Only 3,000 employers in the country are providing child-care support. On-site day care centers, which are the focus of so much media attention, are located in 200 corporate settings and 500 hospitals. Another 800 firms utilize contractors which refer employees to existing child-care providers in their areas. The remainder of the support takes the form of flexible spending accounts, in which the worker can utilize pretax salary to pay for child care.[25]

Sixty percent of women in the work force have no job-protected leave after childbirth.[26] Most major corporations have developed policies, but small businesses have not followed suit and are lobbying actively against any government-mandated leave. Paid parental leave is almost nonexistent. At best, the employee is allowed to use her own leave and supplement it with unpaid leave if possible.

It is unlikely that business will be able to ignore working mothers indefinitely. By the year 2000, women will compose 47 percent of the work force and most of them will become pregnant during their working lives. In the next decade, women will constitute 60 percent of new entrants into the labor force. The majority of these women will be mothers of small children.[27]

Many corporations are taking the lead in providing child-care support, parental leave, and other types of assistance. Recognizing that there is no magic barrier which separates an employee's professional and private life, these firms recognize that fragmented, worried parents do not make productive workers.

Some programs which have been successful are parent resource centers, phone hotlines to aid latchkey children, flexible benefit plans which offer additional time off as a choice, child care consortiums, alternative work patterns, etc. I hope that, one day, all of these options will be commonplace and not just in experimental stages.

FEMINISM

Just as women are searching for a workable balance between careers and families, the women's movement is in the midst of a similar crisis in seeking a balanced image for itself. Many voices within the feminist movement are joining those from more traditional female groups, such as the American Association of University Women and the Association of Junior Leagues to call for societal changes to facilitate options for all mothers. Even labor unions have begun to join in the chorus.

There is no doubt that the women's movement has accomplished a great deal in a relatively short time. In a recent Gallup poll, 71 percent of the respondents felt that the movement had improved their lives. Fifty-six percent of those surveyed considered themselves feminists.[28]

At the same time, there is an indisputable anger directed at the women's movement for what it has created and also for what it has ignored. This anger comes from both sides of the fence. Homemakers feel betrayed that their choice seems somehow less of an option than that of their employed sisters. Joslin, 42, left her teaching career to raise two daughters (introduced on p. 78). She is now attending graduate school and planning the rest of her life. She definitely feels that society is pushing her to get back to work.

"I started feeling the pressure of society a couple of years ago. I felt that the women's movement started out by saying, 'You have a choice as to whether you go back to work or stay

home.' Then I got the feeling that if you didn't choose going
to work you were wasting your time and that there was something
wrong with you.

"When I chose to stay home when my children were little,
society was accepting that. Now I'm feeling that society is saying,
'You better do more with your life than just stay at home with
your children.' "

"Superwomen" are complaining, too. Almost every issue
of any woman's magazine today carries a testimony from a high-
powered female executive in her late thirties or early forties
who is giving it all up to stay home with the children. They
assert that you can not do it all and that feminists have sold
them a bill of goods.

Lisa, 31, left her job as a pediatric nurse practitioner to
be home with her daughter (introduced on p. 93). She does
not want to remain a homemaker indefinitely. Nor does she
want to put too much energy into a career while her daughter
is young.

"Society has not made it easy for women who stay home.
. . . The women's liberation movement tried to make it easier
for women to make a choice, to go back to work or to stay home.
I think they made it harder for women at home. I don't think
they intentionally wanted to do that, but they did.

"I think they've seen that now. They've seen how hard it's
been for women who have tried to do everything, the
Superwoman. . . . Many of these career women have even had
to give up families. They've delayed childbearing and found out
that the biological timeclock has run out. They get to the point
where they say, 'What am I doing all of this for?' They want
to be able to give something to somebody else and now they're
not able to do that."

Some women identify very strongly with feminist principles
and consider it their duty to further the movement's goals
through their choices. They aspire to nonsexist childraising and
household management. They also seek to present a positive
female role model, showing that women can do all sorts of
jobs, not necessarily through paid employment.

A former colleague of mine was a dedicated feminist. She
considered it imperative to be employed so that her two young
daughters would not see her as "just a mother." After analyzing
her financial situation, she discovered that it was actually costing
her money to work as a part-time career counselor for a women's
organization. I was amused when she told me that she had left
her job to become a family day care provider. She was making
a lot more money as a substitute mother than as a career woman!

At least one of the feminist founders has become quite outspoken in identifying a new feminine mystique, this time belonging to working women. Betty Friedan has written about a new generation of women now competing for success according to the male model in a work world fashioned for men who had wives to tend to the details of home life.[29] These women feel entitled to have it all and expect to perform in all areas perfectly. They often end up with frustration, disappointment, guilt, and a sense of failure. Like homemakers a generation ago, they feel that they are the problem and that they are alone.

Friedan sees the futility of women individually attempting to solve work and family problems. She issues a rallying call for another movement to address restructuring work (parental leave, alternative work patterns, etc.) and home (housekeeping patterns, family responsibilities, etc.). Young women should feel entitled to the opportunities afforded them, but recognize that while there are good choices in the working world now, women do not yet have good choices about having children.[30]

YOUR EQUATION

The issues you should consider and may want to include in the societal portion of your equation are the following:

- How much does the media's portrayal of your career choice affect you?
- Do you feel pressure to provide a lot of things or experiences for your family to keep up with others?
- How much support do you get from society of your choice?
- Do you expect societal changes that will help you before your children are grown?
- Is there any group or philosophy with which you identify strongly and feel that your work choice should confirm your beliefs?

FOOTNOTES

[1]National Commission on Working Women, "Commission Releases 'Prime Time Kids'," *Women at Work* (Fall, 1985), p. 1.

[2]*Ibid.*

[3]Betty Friedan, *The Second Stage* (New York: Summit Books, 1981), p. 74.

[4]Claudia Wallis, "The Child-Care Dilemma," *Time* (June 22, 1987), 129:25, p. 58.

[5]*Ibid.*

[6]Sheila B. Kamerman, Alfred J. Kahn and Paul Kingston, *Maternity Policies and Working Women* (New York: Columbia University Press, 1983), p. 15.

[7]*Ibid.*

[8]"Stress and the Working Parent," *Work Times* (Winter, 1986), 4:2, p. 7.

[9]Friedan, *op. cit.,* p. 120.

[10]Office of Congresswoman Pat Schroeder, "Fact Sheet on Parental and Disability Leave Act of 1985," p. 1.

[11]Maria E. Reico, "Should Business Be Forced to Help Bring Up Baby?" *Business Week* (April 6, 1987), #2992, p. 39.

[12]Diane Weathers, "The Superwoman Squeeze," *Newsweek* (May 19, 1980), 95:20, p. 76.

[13]Bureau of the Census, U.S. Department of Commerce, "Trends in Child Care Arrangements of Working Mothers," *Current Population Reports* (June, 1982), P-23, No. 117, p. 32.

[14]Sheila B. Kamerman and Alfred J. Kahn, *Child Care, Family Benefits and Working Parents* (New York: Columbia University Press, 1981), p. 37.

[15]*Ibid.,* p. 41.

[16]*Ibid.*

[17]*Ibid.,* p. 45.

[18]Bureau of the Census, *op. cit.,* p. 36.

[19]Weathers, *op. cit.,* p. 76.

[20]Wallis, *op. cit.,* p. 60.

[21]*Ibid.*

[22]Kamerman and Kahn, *op. cit.,* p. 218.

[23]"A Mother's Choice," *Newsweek* (March 31, 1986), 107:13, pp. 47, 57.

[24]Jeanne Mager Stellman, *Women's Work, Women's Health* (New York: Pantheon Books, 1977), p. 204.

[25]Dana E. Friedman, "Work vs. Family: War of the Worlds," *Personnel Administrator* (August, 1987), 32:8, p. 28.

[26]*Ibid.*

[27]Shirley Dennis, "Is Work a Family Affair?" *Personnel Administrator* (August, 1987), 32:8, p. 51.

[28]"A Mother's Choice," *op. cit.,* p. 5.

[29]Betty Friedan, "Where Do We Go from Here?" *Working Woman* (November, 1986), p. 152.

[30]*Ibid.*

12.
The Big Answer

Making a decision involves both a rational analysis of the issues as well as dealing with your emotions. Most people will not choose more than one answer at a time. Not altering your current situation is indeed still making a decision. You must choose one or more of the following:

- Unemployment;
- Permanent part-time employment;
- Full-time employment;
- Free-lance or consulting work;
- Owning your own business;
- Leave of absence.

Although some women may have peculiar circumstances which dictate their choices, for most of us, the "inputs" for our decisions will fall under the major areas that we have discussed:

- Financial considerations;
- Professional and personal goals;
- Impact upon your child;
- Degree of support from spouse, relatives, friends, and neighbors;
- Societal influences.

If you have written out an equation, take a while to review it and ponder the points you have noted. Look at the big picture first. Does the information direct you to a particular choice?

Next, circle any comments or inputs which represent

163

extremely strong feelings on your part. Do these emotional issues confirm what the equation says? If so, you have a clear choice. Do the emotional issues contradict the results of a rational analysis? If so, the two must be resolved somehow.

For instance, "Mary" has just had a baby and needs to work to supplement her family's income. She is a professional whose career would be adversely affected if she were to drop out of the work force for a long period of time. She does not believe that her child would be damaged by alternative child care. However, she believes it is best for him to have a parent at home at least for the first year. Mary is nursing her baby and finds the thought of turning him over to someone else for long periods to be emotionally wrenching. Her husband says he will support her, regardless of her decision. What should she do?

Here are some possible options:

- *If* the family can forego her income temporarily and *if* she can work out an extended leave from her job, Mary can stay home until she is finished nursing and/or ready to explore child-care possibilities.

- *If* she can work out an arrangement to work part time, Mary can partially meet conflicting needs.

- Mary can quit her job and worry about the future later. Since her income is necessary, the family must either go deeper in debt or change spending patterns in order to survive on one income.

- Mary can return to her job full time and see if the separation from her child is as bad as she anticipates.

None of these answers is "right." However, one of them is best for Mary and that is the decision she must make. Furthermore, some of the possible alternatives are not fully within her control, so Mary must depend upon the cooperation of others. When the head and the heart are in conflict, no choice is going to be perfect. The most that you can hope for is "the best under the circumstances."

TOMORROW

Few answers are good for all time. When my son was two years old, the accumulation of baby paraphernalia forced us out of our first home. I began househunting with the intent to find a home where we could raise our family for the next twenty years. In addition, I wanted a house that could accommodate changes in the family: another child or two, the possibility of one or both of my parents moving in with us in the future, and maybe an office in the home.

It did not take me long to figure out that I was trying to accomplish the impossible. I could not find a house that would be perfect for twenty years. The best I could do was to find something that met our current needs, giving some thought to which changes might occur in the foreseeable future.

We ended up buying what I call our "little kid" house. Our home is on a cul-de-sac with sidewalks, which have been circled many times by tricycles, Big Wheels, bikes and now, skateboards. Bedrooms are on the main floor which I estimate has saved me a few hundred miles of walking up and down stairs to attend to the needs of little ones. We have a small living room and dining room; who has time to entertain? The kitchen is huge, and is the center of much family activity. There is a playroom downstairs where many children's toys are kept. I do not see the mess; hence, it does not bother me.

Soon, we may outgrow this house. The sidewalks will no longer be necessary. Now, the children are civilized enough to be allowed in all of the rooms of a house. We probably will not need the big kitchen and I won't miss scrubbing the floor. I want a master bedroom suite, preferably on another floor from the children's bedrooms, and a larger recreation room more suitable to teenagers. Finally, I will need a large living room for my baby grand piano, which I have not yet figured out how to finance.

Despite my dreams or anticipations of the future, I will not be able to make a decision until the time comes. I can not predict what our financial status will be. I do not even know for certain how many people will be living in the house. What I think I want now may be entirely different from what I actually want when it is time to make a decision.

Making a choice to work or not while raising your family is very similar. The future should not be ignored. However, it should not be planned for nor worried about to the extent that it makes "today" miserable. I spoke to women who were so concerned about what would or might happen to them or their children, that it impaired their abilities to do the best thing now. On the other hand, I found many others who could not see past the circumstances of the present and had not given one thought to how their current choices would affect their futures.

CHANGE OF COURSE

Quite often, I feel overwhelmed by big decisions. Being extremely analytical by nature, I explore every possibility with all its conceivable consequences. I remember spending three sleepless months while deciding whether or not to withdraw my son from our neighborhood public school with which I was not pleased. In explaining my dilemma to a friend, I got into the pros and cons of the public school system, educational philosophies, social considerations, financial investment, etc. After patiently listening to me, she shrugged her shoulders and said, "You're not happy; try something else and see if it's any better. You can always move him back." How simple! It helped me to realize I was affecting a year of his life, not necessarily his entire educational future.

Decisions do not need to be set in concrete. The possibility of changing course should ameliorate a difficult choice. You can always go back to the fork in the road and try another path. You may not get as far along on the path. Furthermore, lost time can not be recaptured. Some options may actually disappear. However, usually there is some alternative. If things are not working out, recognize it and do something to improve the situation.

We have met many women who have changed directions regarding work choices. Neva (introduced on p. 48) began a part-time work schedule after the birth of her second child. It has worked out so well for her that she wishes she had tried it when her first son was born. The switch from homemaker to full-time employment had many positive effects for Diane and her family (introduced on p. 38). Her main complaint is that there is just not enough time for herself and her family and she wishes she could work out a four-day workweek.

Part-time work does not provide the proper balance for all women. Rosanne was thankful for the added time that part-time jobs allowed her to have with her children (introduced on p. 31). Once they were past the infant stage, she found that the schedule was fragmenting to both her and the children. In addition, her part-time status did not allow her the rapid career advancement or salary that she wanted. For Joy, a part-time job was too much (introduced on p. 29). She now regrets the substitute teaching she did after her first child was born. The job and the money were not worth the problems of balancing work and family responsibilities to her.

After years of juggling three children and a full-time job, Susan decided she could no longer manage (introduced on p. 38). Her leave of absence was both a trial run at full-time motherhood and an opportunity to sort out other possible solutions. Many homemakers like Marie come to a point where they feel less needed by their children (introduced on p. 80). Working, part time or full time, can fill that void and create new interests for the woman.

Work decisions are often the result of trial and error. Experiencing the pros and cons of a particular work choice is more valuable than guessing what it will be. Finding the right balance may only come after trying a couple of different options.

A change in direction can be beneficial to all concerned. Possibly circumstances have altered so that the "old choice" is no longer valid. Perhaps you simply have gotten tired of the decision you have made. The major danger of change is when there is too much of it in too short a time. Major changes are disruptive, even when they are positive. They should be thought out carefully.

AND THEY LIVED HAPPILY EVER AFTER

Wise decisions do not guarantee happy endings. Changes, unforeseen circumstances, unexpected reactions, etc., can all create snags in the smooth execution of a plan. Sometimes the logistics of choice simply will prove to be impossible. Maddening as it may seem, there are plenty of people who take huge steps operating on nothing but instinct, and many of them succeed.

One of the interview questions was, "Looking back over the choices you've made regarding work and family issues, which decision(s), if any, would you change if you could?" A few happy souls replied without a moment's hesitation, "Nothing!" However, most of the women would have done something differently.

Even those who were happy with their choices expressed some regret that it was not easier to "have it all." Alice, 32, has obtained a graduate degree and worked intermittently at part-time jobs in the last eleven years (introduced on p. 60). She is always looking out for a job, but has not yet found something interesting and lucrative enough to disrupt her current activities. She has no regrets about her choice to stay home.

"After I had Dawn, I had an opportunity to work. I had looked into day care and I just could not leave her. This was the baby I wanted; we were now a family and I just decided to put that on hold rather than pay someone else to do what I would enjoy doing. I was extremely happy I made that decision.

. . . it really bonded us. . . . I constantly reassess the situation
and see where I'm going with it."

Many of the women said they probably would have made
the same decision at that point in time, but given the way their
lives have developed, they occasionally regret certain choices.
Suzie, 37, chose to be a homemaker years before her children
were born (introduced on p. 52). She is now separated from
her husband and working part time. Part of his dissatisfaction
with the marriage was that they were not "growing" in the
same ways. She inferred that her lack of a paid, professional
career was greatly responsible for these sentiments.

"I probably would have gone back to part-time work or
college sooner. I would have gotten out of the house sooner,
on a part-time basis. I don't know what direction I would have
gone in, but I would not have consumed myself so much with
being a full-time mother."

Marilyn, 47, sees financial pressure as the main inhibitor
to making decisions that may have been best for her (introduced
on p. 152). She and her husband are both committed to his
ministry with high-school youth. Because his salary is low, and
sometimes not even paid, her income is crucial to the family.
She has chosen an assortment of paraprofessional jobs which
give her the flexibility to help her husband and keep up with
the many activities of her three children.

"There are times in my fantasies when I wish money weren't
an issue. Basically, I've liked what I've done and our children
have not been deprived. . . . If the need (for money) weren't
always so strong, I might take more time to find the ideal thing
for me to do. I always end up with plenty of options, but I
take them on an expedient basis. . . . If money weren't such
an issue, I might take six months to decide or I might take some
specific courses to give me the credentials that might change
the kind of work I do."

Of the noncircumstantial regrets expressed, two overwhelming patterns emerged. Both have a common thread, of not
realizing or appreciating how long your life is (hopefully) and
that these work and family conflicts will consume a much shorter
time span than it seems when you are in the midst of it.
Furthermore, the intense period of problems and conflict occur
primarily when the children are young.

The biggest regret expressed by working women, both part
time and full time, was succumbing to the pressure and rush

to "do it all" in such a short period of time. The older their children got, the more they realized that there was an end to the period of huge demands by their offspring, and yet the Social Security check was still a long way off. This sentiment was voiced by new mothers struggling as they returned to work, as well as veteran Superwomen with close to two decades of juggling expertise. Below is a sample of comments from working women:

"If I had it to do over again, I would take it easier. I would be less intense. . . . I would spend more time getting where I am. I'm only 43 next month and I've already had two very fulfilling careers. It may have been better if I had taken a little longer to get where I was going. I was always in such a rush."

"Almost everyone expected me to go back to work. I felt pressure. . . . It was probably a mistake to accept that initial job. I wasn't ready yet. I was deep down hoping I wouldn't find the right babysitter so I could refuse the job. It was just not the right time. I wasn't happy with the job, the babysitter — it all didn't work. But I didn't want it to work."

"I wish I had been able to enjoy my kids more and not been so intent upon being a career person. . . . I've really enjoyed my third child more because I've been more relaxed about my career. . . . I think I might have taken out more time and enjoyed them and gotten back into this (career) later. I should have been willing to take a break. I could never see that it was such a short period of time. It seemed like an eternity when I first had kids."

Conversely, the biggest regret voiced by women who chose to remain at home for substantial lengths of time was being too preoccupied with children and failing to plan for future employment. Most women currently at home with children under eighteen do not plan on remaining unemployed after their children are grown. Many plan to return to work when their last child enters school. This leaves twenty to thirty years in the labor force, much longer than the period prior to having children. Below is a sample of comments from homemakers or former homemakers:

"I should have realized early on that a career was important to me. Because I didn't when we first got married. I worked until we had kids and then I thought that would be it. I didn't realize that a job, a career, was important to me. And I wish I had known that sooner."

"I don't regret staying home, but once they were almost raised, it was time to do something more. . . . It's been very

frightening going back to work. . . . I wish I had developed
some skills while I was home. Maybe I should have taken some
courses. Then I could have been more employable later."

"A major regret for me was not completing school and getting
my degree before I had the children. I wouldn't say that I'm
adamant, but my daughter absolutely knows that that is what
I want her to do. . . . Not having a degree has caused a lot
of insecurities for me that I'm still gradually working through."

Possibly these women were merely gazing at grass which
appeared to be greener on the other side of the fence. Maybe
they were not satisfied with the outcomes of their decisions
because they invested too heavily in one area. Perhaps the right
balance just eluded them. The regrets expressed may be an
indication of the tendency to look over our shoulders at what
we did wrong, instead of all we did right.

Many of the women were unhappy with their answers, but
were not sure they really would have done anything differently
at the time. Some felt that they had been born too soon, before
sufficient societal change which might have made their choices
easier. One woman wistfully commented:

"I think for both my husband and myself, I wish there were
more choices for both of us. I wish the entire burden were not
on his shoulders; to educate all these children and to be a money
machine. I wish he could have more of what I had and I could
have a little more of what he had. I hope for my daughter's
generation that that may get worked out a little more so that
she might have more of a choice to leave the house and her
husband might have more of a choice to stay home if he wanted
to."

PERSONAL REFLECTIONS

I approached the big choice personally with two strong beliefs
which were diametrically opposed. They were:

- All things being equal, in our society, a woman with my
  professional background would be unwise to stay home for
  a long period of time unless she were willing (and could afford)
  to consider her career optional.

- All things being equal, children (particularly until school age)
  benefit from heavy parental involvement and limited, but
  slowly increasing amounts of exposure to other people and
  situations.

Those are my biases. They were my "gut feelings" before
I spent ten years researching this topic. Nothing I have learned

in the intervening time has altered my prejudices dramatically. However, I recognize that for most people, all things are not equal. There are circumstances, beliefs, personality traits, talents, and problems which often make things quite unequal.

In the last ten years, my employment has ranged from zero to 50 hours per week. I have experimented with many of the options outlined in Chapter Four. My prevailing decision over these "mothering" years has been to work part time. I recently accepted a full-time job and I have not had sufficient time to analyze the choice. I will share with you some of the major influencing factors of these decisions as viewed through the big equation.

Finance

My income is not necessary for my family's survival, but it allows us to do things and make choices that would be difficult otherwise. At this point, we would have to make some real adjustments if my income disappeared.

I consider it extremely important to be able to support my family if necessary. A paycheck adds to my sense of independence and self-esteem. It would be very difficult for me not to have money "of my own." My husband and I maintain accounts for family expenses as well as accounts for personal spending. This, I believe, is responsible for the fact that we have never had a fight about money in fifteen years of marriage.

The bottom line of my financial equation shows that it is advantageous to work for the amount of money I clear. I will reap a much greater financial benefit when child care expenses disappear.

Because my husband is self-employed, a critical part of my compensation package is employee benefits. My job provides needed health insurance to our family, inexpensive life and disability insurance for me, membership in a retirement system, and a deferred compensation program. The value of the benefits I receive is more than one-quarter of my salary.

Self: Professionally

My occupational background and skills do not allow me to pop in and out of the work force with ease. My experience after taking off nearly two years to obtain a graduate degree and have a baby convinced me that it was not easy to find a job if you did not already have one. As the mother of a young child, it was even harder. My observations of women reentering the labor market after many years of absence is that it is extremely difficult to find a good, professional job and that one rarely can make up totally for the lost time.

Working part time allowed me more time with my family and a degree of flexibility much needed given the amount of activities with which we are involved. Juggling three part-time professional commitments this past year was frantic and tiring, but also interesting and challenging.

I am well aware of the fact that had I concentrated on any one of the areas on a full-time basis for ten years, I would be "further along" in that field. However, I am happy with my current job, enjoy my work, and look forward to future professional growth.

Self: Personally

I am a reasonably happy and contented individual with a very positive self-image. While I operate well under pressure, I often do not recognize the level of stress in my life until I have overdone it and end up in bed sick for a few days. As I mature, I'm attempting to be more sensitive to my aging body's signals and take it easier. However, I admit to being extremely hung up on sticking to schedules and deadlines.

It was not until I had children that I can say I honestly understood the meaning of the word "guilt." My head recognizes that my decisions are not the only influences on their lives, but I often agonize as if they were. Thanks to part-time jobs and a participating father, until this past year, they have spent no more time in alternative child care than if I had chosen to stay home. We maintain a commitment to them for them to spend no more than two days per week at a sitter's house. Therefore, I do not have much "excess guilt baggage" to carry around with me. There are still moments when I get a twinge if I can't go on a field trip, do not have time for a board game, or am doing a lousy job helping with homework at the end of a long day.

My Children

I think my children have benefitted from a more equal amount of time from both parents. We have been fortunate in having good babysitters and excellent nursery schools. Each of the children participate in a variety of activities which call for heavy time commitments and plenty of carpools. I am sure they would like to have their parents available all day, every day at their disposal. With some fear and trepidation I interviewed my children, asking each of them what he or she thought about

Mom working. (This was before my recent job switch.)
    From Tara, age 5:

Q: Can you think of any moms who have jobs?

A: Everybody's mom has a job. (Most of her friends' mothers are employed.)

Q: What is my job?

A: You write books. (That's all she sees.)

Q: Do you know what I do in my offices?

A: No.

Q: What does Daddy do?

A: He mails things.

Q: What is he called?

A: A lawyer. He gets people out of jail.

Q: Why do I work?

A: To get money.

Q: Any other reasons?

A: So you can buy things.

Q: Any other reasons?

A: Not that I know of.

Q: Do you think it's good that I have a job?

A: YES. So you can get money. If you didn't work, you wouldn't get money, right?

Q: What are some of the good things about Mommy working, besides getting money?

A: Buying things — like food and a house.

Q: Are there any bad things?

A: No.

Q: Nothing?

A: No.

Q: Don't you miss me when I'm at work?

A: Yes. (I really had to drag that out!)

Q: Isn't that a bad thing?

A: Yes.

Q: Do you like school and going to the babysitter's house?

A: Yeah.

Q: When you grow up, do you think you'd like to have a job while you're a mom?

A: Let me see, a part-time job, not full time.

Q: Would you want it to be part time forever or until your children go to school?

A: I don't know.

My daughter obviously is destined for a career in banking. My son, Brian, showed considerably more insight at age 9:

Q: Do you know what my job is?

A: You work for Part-Time Professionals.

Q: How about the job I go to where I leave early in the morning?

A: Oh yeah, you work for the government.

Q: Do you know what I do there?

A: You pay taxes.

Q: What else?

A: You're writing four books.

Q: Why do I work?

A: So you can get money.

Q: Any other reasons?

A: You like it.

Q: Why do you think I like it?

A: You get hamburgers for lunch. (I once made the mistake of telling him I go through a fast-food drive-in on Wednesdays, the day I go to two offices.)

Q: Any other reasons?

A: Because you're interviewed a lot on TV and at one of the jobs, you get to be your own boss.

Q: Do you think it's good that I have jobs?

A: Yes, we have more money and then we can go places, like Florida, North Carolina, and Hong Kong. (We have never been to Hong Kong.)

Q: Are there any bad things?

A: We miss you.

Q: Thank you. (That child stays in the will.) Anything else?

A: You can't always get stuff done around the house and you have to pay babysitters.

Q: If I could quit my job tomorrow, should I do it?

A: No, then we'd have to move to an apartment or a condominium.

Q: When you get married and have children, do you want your wife to work?

A: Not until they're three. Then they can go to preschool. Until then, she has to stay home and guard the babies so they don't run off. She can work at home if she wants, like painting or something.

Q: Well, what if they went to a sitter's, like Miss Claudine. Would that be alright?

A: Yeah, if Miss Claudine would want to do it.

Q: When the children go to preschool, do you want your wife to work?

A: Yes.

Q: How come?

A: So we can support the family.

Q: What if you end up rich, do you still want her to work?

A: No, then she could stay home.

Q: What would she do at home?

A: She could clean the house and make my lunch and dinner. If I made a lot of money, we really wouldn't need to have two people work.

Q: What if your wife were real rich, would you like to stay home?

A: No, I'd be bored. But that's what women do. Men aren't made for it; women are.

I think I fainted dead away at that point.

My Husband

My husband is a wise man. He will give opinions when asked, but his basic attitude toward my employment has been, "It's your decision, and I'll support you in whatever your choice is." Who can fight with that?

His support has been active in that he takes responsibility for child care and household functions which allow me to pursue professional opportunities. He does more than most men I know and his participation is facilitated by his self-employment. It is also a fact that if I took over most of these responsibilities, he would let me. He does not do grocery shopping, cook meals, and run carpools because he loves it. It is because of a sense of fairness and a wife who constantly discusses how *we* will handle responsibilities.

My Relatives, Friends, and Neighbors

I must confess that none of these categories weigh heavily enough in my equation to alter my choice. I am grateful for their support and probably do not deal with other reactions. Not one person has ever directly told me that I should quit a job or work more.

My mother, once she determined that her only grandchildren were not suffering, has confined her anxiety to my physical well-being, in light of my hectic schedule. I do not think my father quite understands why I work. However, he is interested in what I do and is a source of good advice. My sister is a single, working woman who I doubt comprehends the big choice. She merely would like me to "take it easy" occasionally.

I have friends who have chosen a variety of options for a variety of reasons. Their support is felt in terms of their respect for my decision as well as cooperative efforts at carpooling and babysitting.

As mentioned previously, my neighborhood has few women at home. For this reason, it is not a place that I would be happy to be home on a full-time basis. I am sure I would feel very lonely.

Society

I feel that most areas of society have done extremely little to aid me in my attempts to balance career and family commitments. I feel fortunate to have an employer that makes job-sharing and part-time opportunities available. Most mothers do not have the option of a part-time professional position as I did with my first government position. It angers me that alternatives like this are not available to more people and that it has been so difficult to get where I am.

I confess to being as influenced by our materialistic, image-conscious society as anyone else, and wage a daily battle to keep my priorities in line with my beliefs and make wise decisions about what is really best for me and the people I love.

The social and political forces I support recognize my right to pursue personal career goals, while not weakening the strength of the family.

MY WISH

I would have done many things differently before I had children if I had known the basic dilemma that was to face me in the coming years. Primarily, I would have made career choices which would have lessened the problems of combining career and mothering roles. Children do not raise themselves and if you put any kind of effort into effective parenting, they do influence your career. Furthermore, they need you at unannounced times, not just when you have decided to schedule quality time.

Having made very few wise decisions before the issue of work and family conflicts became apparent, I had to invest time and energy into making the best of my resources. I believe that I have made wise choices which have been best for all concerned. This did not happen by chance, but by work.

My wish for you is the same. Take responsibility for your life and its outcome. Do the work and take the time to resolve the big choice. There are a limited amount of options. The inputs are there for you to analyze. Be objective, yet do not ignore strong emotions. Once you have done it, relax and enjoy! And when it does not seem to work out well, do it again!

13.
A Legacy for Our Daughters

In the last twenty years, we have witnessed near revolutionary social upheaval regarding the family and women's role in society. What will the next twenty years bring? If and when my daughter begins a family, I pray that she will not even face the big choice and that alternative options for raising children and maintaining a career will be available and accepted. Furthermore, I want my son to have the same options and for them to be equally socially acceptable.

I believe that if this change does occur, it will be as a result of economic circumstances, not social goodwill. For many years now, the largest growing portion of the labor force has been women with children under six. This expanding segment of the work force will make its needs known in business, government, and labor unions. Secondly, due to demographic changes, our country will be facing labor shortages in some fields as early as the 1990s, with more critical problems coming in many areas after the turn of the century. Employers will be more receptive to workers' needs in order to attract and retain their employees.

Young women today are increasingly more aware of the career options that are available to them and just how important their occupational choices are. Unfortunately, many of these same individuals are naive enough to believe that jobs and babies present no real dilemma and that combining career and family duties is a natural and easy process.

There is some evidence that how women view combining a career and family affects their early choices. One study of adolescents revealed that the girls first decided how they would combine the two roles of worker and parent, and which one would get priority. This decision often directly affected their choices of careers. High-prestige jobs were frequently eliminated from consideration because they were perceived as requiring too high a degree of commitment.[1]

This same study showed that the adolescent girls were far more affected by "significant others" in their career choices than their male counterparts. As the young women came closer to an age of marriage and job decisions, their perceptions of the difficulty in finding marital partners affected career choices. The young women often moderated career goals in accordance with men's wishes, while the reverse was rarely true.[2]

Many women of my generation have felt unprepared for the necessity of earning a living long term and equally unskilled in the area of combining career and family responsibilities. This can hardly be blamed upon our mothers, most of whom fully expected us to live lives identical to their own. How will our children look back at what we have given them? What will their childhood memories be? Can we anticipate and prepare them for the future any better than our own parents did?

No one disputes the fact that increased choices for women and the growing numbers of working mothers have dramatically affected the family. Most view the changes as mixed blessings, with sacrifices and benefits for all concerned. Careers outside the home can be exciting for some women, offering self-esteem and a sense of independence. These women feel they can contribute to the family's well-being in diverse ways. On the other hand, too much responsibility results in exhaustion, leaving women ineffectual in any arena. Many jobs (at home and in the office) are not exciting in the least. One woman summed it up by saying, "Happy mothers are good mothers and wives, regardless of whether or not they work outside the home."

Many women expressed a desire to relieve their husbands of total financial responsibility for the family, particularly if this could free time for them to be more participative family members. One woman who had worked full time and also had stayed at home felt her marriage was stronger during the working years.

"Working helps the relationship with your spouse because you're on equal terms. If you're both working, you both realize the pressure the other is under. If one is home and one is employed, you are basically operating in two different worlds, unless you somehow have a lot of extra time to communicate.

When you get to the children, it depends on what kind of day care you have and also on how much time they have to be there. There are just pros and cons on both sides and it depends on so many factors like money, job, child care, etc."

Many women I meet express a real concern about the family life we are providing for our children. Many think that children are suffering, while women and marriages are doing better. They don't want to rectify the situation by turning back the clock thirty years, but by providing supports to all families — regardless of their choices.

I interviewed a teacher of emotionally disturbed children who credits many of the problems she sees in the school to unstable home environments. She personally has a changing work schedule which means that her first-grade son must remember which days to walk home or go to a babysitter's house. She feels that this is an unfair burden for him when she always knew her mother would be home after school.

There are also those who credit working women with destroying family life. One of my interviewees stated:

> "Working women have affected family life tremendously negatively. . . . Moms and dads are often gone when they're needed. Children end up watching television and doing things that may not have a positive impact (upon them).
>
> When mother comes home at night, she's too tired to talk. Family activities decrease. . . . We have a value system based on things which pass away . . . on experiences, things, freedom, doing what feels good, not on relationships. Children suffer tremendously when Mother works."

Many women simply acknowledge the tradeoffs and admit that they have no idea what the bottom line will be. One woman admitted that her part-time employment was a way of "hedging her bet."

> "For the woman, she's been offered a choice. Society has become more accepting of working mothers. . . . (We don't know) how it's affecting the family because this is the first generation to have a majority of working mothers.
>
> By working part time and going down the middle of the road, I hope that if they find out in 50 years that the family structure has been destroyed, then I guess I'll only have half-destroyed my family. I don't think that will be the case. I think we'll come up with more effective alternatives."

We definitely need to come up with alternatives to this and other tangential social concerns, such as the manner in which we administer community and volunteer activities. Volunteers are disappearing in direct proportion to female labor force expansion. Nonprofit organizations which have depended upon a volunteer base for existence find their membership, staff, and budgets shrinking at alarming rates. Brownie leaders, room mothers, PTA officers, and volunteer political activists are scarce commodities.

Many worthwhile activities can be saved by altering times of operation to accommodate families with hectic schedules. Others will only continue through payment for services received by charging the consumers of those services. Creative alternatives are essential because of a small proportion of individuals are assuming an unfair burden for many of these very important activities.

ADVICE FROM MOM

Just in case they ask, and even more surprisingly, if they listen, what advice will we give our daughters regarding work and family choices? If current trends continue, most of our daughters will spend a majority of their active parenting years also bringing in a paycheck.

I suppose the first type of advice would concern the timing of becoming a parent. A recent magazine article outlined the pros and cons of taking the parenting plunge early or late in a career. There is no "right" time and a common childbearing age span (25 to 35 years of age) coincides with a period of rapid career growth.

For those who have their families at a young age:

- It is easier to conceive.

- They have more energy to deal with the dual demands from children and employers.

- They sacrifice less money if they drop out of the work force because they are not yet earning high salaries.

- An uninterrupted career awaits once children are not longer as dependent.

- The family must survive on less money if full-time work is not continued.

For those who delay childbearing until careers are well established:

- They build up greater financial security.

- They may be more inclined to relax, settle down and enjoy their children.

- Flexible work options are more of a possibility because the women are more likely to be in positions with some power.

- The golden years may be burdensome with college tuition, elderly parents, and retirement.[3]

Once our grandchildren do arrive, what would we like to see our daughters do? Many of the women I interviewed would advise their offspring to follow in their footsteps. It was not always apparent to me if this counsel was a result of being pleased with the outcome of a decision or the desire for an insecure choice to be reinforced. Below are responses from a homemaker, a part-time employed woman and a full-time employed woman:

> "My daughter has expressed interest in having about nine children, and I've told her she won't need another career. If she wants to have a career, she should do that before or after she has her children. . . . If she chooses to get married and have children, she should just do that and not worry about a career. It will come later if that's what she wants."

> "I have a history of working part time and it's been a wonderful combination. I would advise her to do what I've done, to be only committed (to a job) part time when she has young children, but to definitely do something on a part-time basis. I think it's very difficult to be a good parent when you only are parenting and don't keep your own personal and professional skills alive."

> "My daughter says she wants to work like me when she grows up. . . . I would tell her not to go through a guilt thing; the kids would be okay. Also, don't worry about what other people think, if they question what kind of a mother you are for leaving your children with somebody else. Be secure about yourself."

Overwhelmingly, the most common thread in the advice of mothers to their daughters is to look ahead, be prepared and be established professionally and financially before children enter the picture. This sentiment was expressed in the following thoughts:

- Delay children.
- Complete your education first.
- Work before marriage and children so you know what it's about.
- Have a marketable skill.
- Think ahead and plan a life that will be workable.
- Prepare yourself for all possible circumstances.
- Don't count on being taken care of.

- Choose a career with flexibility.

- Take a job that will work on a part-time basis.

- Look at the consequences of each choice and weigh them carefully.

The second most repeated counsel concerned future sons-in-law. Husbands were acknowledged to be a critical factor in the wife's decision as well as the success of her choice. Some of the advice about husbands follows:

- Marry the right man.

- Tell your husband your goals.

- Be sure your husband assumes responsibility.

- Marry a rich man so you won't have to worry about any of this.

I admire one woman who responded emphatically that she had just as much advice to pass along to her son.

"I've thought a lot about this. I (would) want to be a good example and to let her know what was going on in my thoughts and my life when she was old enough to appreciate the choices that I was making or forced to make. This is also just as important to me for my son because I want him to appreciate womanhood and the choices we have to make. Women have far more choices to make than men and I want him to be compassionate in that respect."

The final common point was made most frequently by older mothers. Their advice was to relax about the big choice. These women generally felt that they had spent too much time and energy anguishing over their actions. Additionally, they felt that in the midst of the turmoil, their perspective of time was warped, magnifying the dilemma and the problems. Regardless of the work status, they wanted to assure their daughters that it was all right not to do everything perfectly and to enjoy the benefits of their decisions while attempting to overcome the disadvantages.

I close with my personal favorite "advice" quote from a mom. I am sure I like it because it expresses some of my own sentiments:

"I think going back part time was the right first step for me. It lets you know whether working is right for you. If it's not, feel comfortable with your decision.

Once you've made a choice and become committed to it, don't continue to question whether it's right or wrong. Realize that you're going to have up-and-down days, and that some days at home will be better than others and some days at work will be better than others.

Be satisfied with the decision you've made. And if it's not working, be smart enough to say, 'I've got to reevaluate this.' But don't rehash something you're satisfied with."

FOOTNOTES

[1] Judy Corder and Cookie White Stephan, "Females, Combination of Work and Family Roles: Adolescents' Aspirations," *Journal of Marriage and the Family* (May, 1984), 46:2, pp. 391–392.

[2] *Ibid.*, p. 392.

[3] Marlys Harris, "The Three-Career Life," *Money* (May, 1985), 14:5, pp. 109–110.

Index

ABOUT THE AUTHOR

Barbara Ensor Cook is a personnel administrator for a local government agency. She has co-authored previous books on employment issues. For eight years, she worked for the Association of Part-Time Professionals, serving as Co-Director and President of the Washington Area Chapter.

Photo by M. Nanette Butler

Throughout her ten years of parenting, the author has experimented with various work options. She has worked at home and in traditional offices, and has had part-time and full-time jobs, job-sharing arrangements, and free-lance assignments. The entire time she has debated "the big choice." She lives in Reston, Virginia with her husband, David, and her children, Brian and Tara.